Author in the field

AFOOT & AFIELD IN

Orange County

Jerry Schad

WILDERNESS PRESS
BERKELEY

FIRST EDITION 1988
Second printing April 1992
Third printing June 1993
Fourth printing April 1995
SECOND EDITION November 1996
Second printing March 1998
Third printing July 2000
Fourth printing August 2002

Photos and maps by the author
Cover photo (large) © 1996 Larry Ulrich
Cover photo (inset) © 1996 Jerry Schad
Design by Kathy Morey and Thomas Winnett
Cover design by Larry B. Van Dyke

Library of Congress Card Catalog Number 96-41708
International Standard Book Number 0-89997-206-3

Manufactured in the United States of America

Published by **Wilderness Press**
            1200 5th Street
            Berkeley, CA 94710
            (800) 443-7227; FAX (510) 558-1696
            mail@wildernesspress.com

            Contact us for a free catalog
            Visit our website at **www.wildernesspress.com**

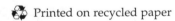 Printed on recycled paper

Cover photo (large): **Surf grass at Pelican Point, Crystal Cove State Park**
Cover photo (inset): **California poppies**

Library of Congress Cataloging-in-Publication Data
Schad, Jerry.
    Afoot and afield in Orange County / Jerry Schad.—2nd ed.
        p.   cm.
    Includes bibliographical references and index.
    ISBN 0-89997-206-3
        1. Hiking—California—Orange County—Guidebooks. 2. Orange County (Calif.)—Guidebooks.
3. Natural history—California—Orange County. I. Title.
GV199.42.C220737   1996
917.94'96—dc20   96-41708
                                                                     CIP

Acknowledgements

Many people have offered their time, talents, and knowledge during the various phases of producing the first edition of this book. I would like to thank Ralph Davis, Beth Davis, Mike Fry, Janet Leavitt, Camille Armstrong, Don Nelson, Genie Rope, René Schad, Walton Scott, Bert Ton, Gene Troxell, John Welch, and Howie Wier for sharing adventures with me on the trail, and for helping with transportation. Several people associated with local parks and preserves and Cleveland National Forest have been of assistance too, among them Bill Bretz, Bruce Buchman, Lee Edwards, Ernie Martinson, Jim Snow, and Jon Wright. Ilse Byrnes provided information about Orange County's regional riding-and-hiking trail system. Cathey Byrd designed the symbols that appear at the top of every trip description. Tom Winnett of Wilderness Press, in his usual meticulous way, superbly edited the text. I also wish to thank my wife, René, for her encouragement, and for putting up with 4 a.m. alarms that summoned me to the crest of the Santa Ana Mountains for many a spectacular sunrise.

During the last several years, I have had the pleasure of re-hiking many familiar routes—and also exploring the 15 new trails added to this current, second edition. For assistance in these endeavors, I wish to thank Bob Birkland, Lee Di Gregorio, Marian Mongar, Sky York and Susan Zahn.

Jerry Schad
El Cajon, California
August 1996

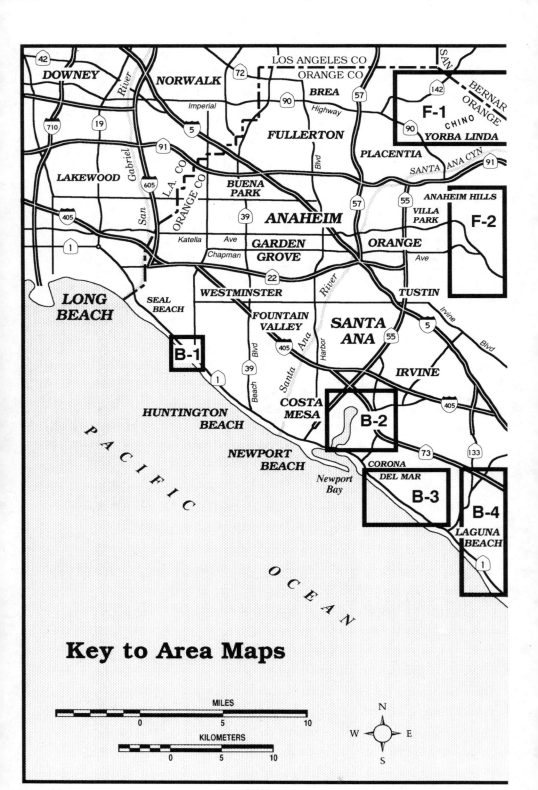

Key to Area Maps

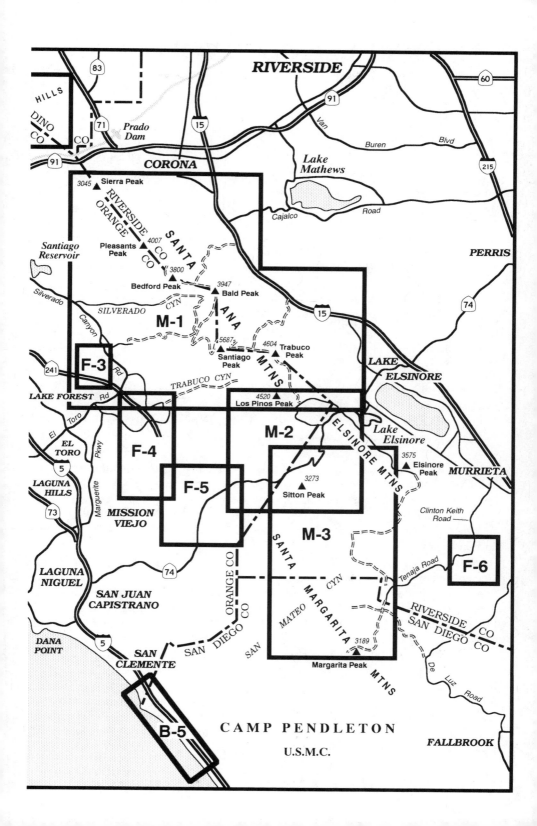

Preface

Hidden within or just beyond Orange County's urban sprawl lies more opportunity for the appreciation of the natural world than most county residents would ever imagine. Barely a few hundred yards from busy highways and shimmering glass highrises, shorebirds haunt protected estuaries and marshes. Along the southern coast, ocean swells roll in and spend themselves against lonely sands and jagged cliffs. Over the foothill country hawks and eagles cruise in search of a furry meal. And deep within the corrugated fastness of the Santa Ana Mountains mountain lions, deer, and coyotes roam cool, dark canyon bottoms and sun-warmed, chaparral-covered slopes.

Surrounding Orange County's densely populated coastal plain are parks, preserves, and public lands totaling nearly 150,000 acres. Within this domain, intriguing pathways introduce explorers to natural landscapes ranging from the intertidal zone to oak and coniferous woodlands. Orange County boasts either within or abutting its rather compact border eight state parks and beaches, 19 regional (county) parks and wilderness areas, more than 130,000 acres of national forest, and more than 400 miles of trails and roads for hiking.

My goal in writing this guide was to bring into sharp focus virtually every walk worth taking on still-wild public lands conveniently accessible to the average Orange Countian. The hikes range in difficulty from short strolls through selected urban parks and preserves to canyon treks in the Santa Ana Mountains that would challenge any adventurer.

Because of Orange County's rather small area (782 square miles) but larger sphere of influence, a number of hikes in this book lie either partly or wholly outside the county boundaries. These are found in the following areas: Chino Hills State Park, extending into San Bernardino and Riverside counties; Santa Rosa Plateau Ecological Reserve in southwestern Riverside County; San Onofre State Beach in northern San Diego County; and the entire Trabuco Ranger District of Cleveland National Forest, spilling into Riverside and San Diego counties. (Two other units of the Cleveland Forest, the Palomar and Descanso districts, extend farther east and south across Riverside and San Diego counties. Those units, along with other public lands in San Diego County, are treated in my book *Afoot and Afield in San Diego County*. For those interested in hikes in and around Los Angeles, a third volume in the "Afoot and Afield" series is available: *Afoot and Afield in Los Angeles County*.)

Every trip in this book was hiked by me at least once at one time or another. Roads and trails can and do change, however. County and state park acreage is increasing, and new trails are being constructed and opened for public use. In the national forest, the greater demand for recreational use is leading to new regulations and new use patterns. I will continue to insert fresh updates in future printings of this edition, and a third edition will undoubtedly appear in the future. You can keep me apprised of recent developments and/or changes by writing me in care of Wilderness Press, 2440 Bancroft Way, Berkeley, CA 94704. I will appreciate your comments.

Contents

New "National Forest Adventure Pass"

In 1997 the national forests of Southern California (Angeles, Cleveland, Los Padres, and San Bernardino) collectively instituted a recreation fee program called the "National Forest Adventure Pass." Vehicles parked along roadsides and at trailheads are now required to display a National Forest Adventure Pass permit, or else risk being ticketed. The permit, which costs $5 daily or $30 yearly, can be purchased from any national forest office or ranger station, and from virtually every Southern California outdoor equipment and sports vendor. The permit is valid in all four of the national forests. In this book, almost all of the trailheads for trips in the "Santa Ana Mountains" section (Areas M-1 through M-3) lie within Cleveland National Forest and therefore require the adventure pass.

Introducing Orange County

From the look-alike cities in the north to the newer, planned communities of the south, Orange County seems little distinguished from its colossal neighbor and economic parent, Los Angeles. But a deeper identity, rooted in geography, transcends the urban sprawl. Orange Countians are reminded of their uniqueness not so much by the human architecture of city and suburb, but rather by the blue Pacific, the green and tawny coastal hills, and the purple wall of the Santa Ana Mountains.

Out on the coastline and up along the foothills and mountains, you may discover for yourself Orange County's place in the natural world. An hour or less of driving and less than two hours' walk will take you from the frenetic city to any of several interesting natural environments, ranging from tide pools to fern-bedecked canyon streams to mountain peaks affording views stretching a hundred miles. You'll discover fascinating rock formations, rich and varied plant life, a healthy population of native animals, and a sense of peace and tranquillity.

In the next few pages of this book, we'll briefly introduce you to the "other" Orange County: its climate, geology, flora, and fauna. Following that, you'll find some notes about safety and courtesy on the trail, and some tips on how to get the most out of this book. After perusing that material, you can dig into the heart of this book—

descriptions of 72 hiking routes from the coast to the Santa Ana Mountains. Happy reading and happy hiking!

Land of Gentle Climates

A succinct summary of Orange County's climate might take the form of just two phrases: "warm and sunny," and "winter-wet, summer-dry." But some variation in climate exists across the county's width from coast to mountain crests. Without resorting to technical classification schemes, let's divide the county into just two climate zones: The coastal zone, extending inland 10–15 miles across the coastal plain and low coastal foothills, is largely under the moderating influence of the Pacific Ocean. This climate is characterized by mild temperatures that are relatively unvarying, both daily and seasonally. Average Fahrenheit temperatures range from the 60s/40s (daily highs/lows) in winter, to 70s/60s in summer. Rainfall averages about 15 inches annually. Overall this climate closely matches the classic "Mediterranean climate" associated with coastal areas along the Mediterranean Sea.

The inland zone, consisting of the Santa Ana Mountains and foothills, experiences somewhat more extreme daily and seasonal temperatures, because it is less influenced by onshore flows of marine air. The higher summits of the Santa Ana Mountains, for example, have average temperatures in the 50s/20s in winter, and the 80s/50s in summer. Precipitation averages about 30 inches annually in the higher Santa Anas, which is just enough to support natural pockets of coniferous and broadleaf trees such as pines, oaks, and maples. Almost every year, some fraction of the precipitation arrives in the form of snow, which briefly blankets the mountain slopes down to an elevation of about 3000 feet.

Despite its reputation for gentle climate, Orange County is occasionally subject to hot, dry winds called "Santa Ana winds" (after Santa Ana Canyon, just north of the Santa Ana Mountains). These winds occur when an air mass moves southwest from a high-pressure area over the interior U.S. out toward Southern California. As the air flows downward toward the coast, it compresses and becomes warm and dry. Low passes in the mountains, or river valleys that act as wind gaps (such as Santa Ana Canyon), funnel these desertlike winds toward the coast. During stronger Santa Anas, common in late summer and fall, Orange County basks under warm, blue skies swept clear of every trace of pollution (except possibly smoke from wildfires). Temperatures along the coast can then reach record high levels; the city of Orange, for example, once recorded a temperature of 119 degrees during a Santa Ana.

Rainfall in Orange County is as erratic as it is slight. On the coastal plain, the annual precipitation has ranged from just 4 inches to a record of 32 inches. Up to 5 inches have fallen on the coastal plain in a single day, and in the Santa Ana Mountains one storm dumped 9 inches in a single night.

By and large, Orange County's balmy, dry climate is remarkably well suited to year-round outdoor activity. Nevertheless, high temperatures, scarcity of water, and/or high smog levels during summer and early fall make that particular period much less desirable for hiking in the inland foothills and mountains. During the other seven or eight months of the year, however, the weather is often ideal.

Reading the Rocks

Of California's many geomorphic (natural) provinces, Orange County claims parts of just two: the Los Angeles Basin and the Peninsular Ranges. The bulk of the county's urbanized area lies in the Los Angeles Basin, while the mostly undeveloped Santa Ana Mountains and the semi-developed San Joaquin Hills belong to the Peninsular Ranges province.

The Los Angeles Basin province extends from the base of the San Gabriel and Santa Monica mountains (part of the Transverse Ranges province) on the north to the base of the Santa Ana Mountains and the San Joaquin Hills on the south. In a geologic context it can be pictured as a huge, deeply folded basin filled to a depth of up to 7 miles by some volcanic material and land-laid sediments, but mostly by sediments of marine origin—sand and mud deposited on the ocean bottom from 80 million years ago to as recently as 1 million years ago.

The Los Angeles Basin area has experienced uplift during the past 1–2 million years, and as this took place the surface of the basin accumulated a layer of terrestrial sediment shed from the surrounding hills and mountains. The basin, in fact, would be still be filling up with sediment today were it not for the flood-control dams and channeled riverbeds that have largely replaced the original meandering Santa Ana, San Gabriel and Los Angeles rivers.

Hikers following this guidebook will discover many interesting and sometimes colorful exposures of marine sedimentary rocks in places like the Chino Hills, the San Joaquin Hills, and the foothills of the Santa Ana Mountains. These sediments, uplifted by a variety of geologic processes, are continuations of the formations that lie deep underground in the center of the Los Angeles Basin.

The marine sediments you will see— sandstone, siltstone, shale, and conglomerate—tend to be rather soft and easily eroded. Along the south coast, where the San Joaquin Hills meet the sea, several wave-cut "marine terraces" are identifiable on the coastal headlands. They exhibit a record of changing sea levels and gradual uplift over the past one or two million years. In many places the terraces themselves are deeply cut by drainage channels—the coastal canyons—which themselves are quite recent features.

The Santa Ana Mountains, along with the San Jacinto Mountains, lie at the northwest tip of the extensive Peninsular Ranges province, stretching south toward the tip of Baja California (the province, in fact, derives its name from Baja's peninsular shape). Each range in this province possesses a core of granitic (granitelike) rock, overlain in many places by a veneer of older metamorphic rocks. Many of the Peninsular Ranges, including the Santa Anas, are raised and tilted fault blocks, typically with steep east escarpments and more gradually inclined western slopes.

As you travel through the Santa Ana Mountains (and their distinctly named subdivisions, the Elsinore and the Santa Margarita mountains), you'll begin to piece together their geologic history. Starting at, say, Caspers Wilderness Park in the foothills and moving up toward the crest of the Santa Anas, you first pass among light-colored marine sedimentary rock formations that were pushed up and tilted by the rise of the mountains to the east. Next comes metamorphic rock of two basic kinds— metasedimentary and metavolcanic. These brown- or gray-colored rocks, roughly 200– 150 million years old, are metamorphosed (changed by heat and pressure) forms of marine sedimentary and volcanic rock that

Contorted shales at foot of bluff south of Little Corona Beach

were plastered against the core of the North American continent some tens of millions of years ago. These rocks were riding on one or more of the earth's tectonic "plates" which were colliding with and being "subducted" (forced under) the western edge of the continent.

Near the crest of the Santa Ana Mountains you find light-colored granitic rocks. Here's the reason: About 100 million years ago, when the subduction process was in full swing, much of the material on the edge of the plate being subducted was melting underground and accumulating in the form of vast pools of magma. Because this magma was less dense than the surrounding materials, it began rising toward the surface. Some escaped through volcanoes, but most of it remained underground long enough to slowly cool and crystallize, forming coarse-grained "plutonic" (generally granitic) rocks. Erosion then nibbled away at the overlying metamorphic rocks, finally exposing—typically in high places—the granitic rocks.

In the southern Santa Anas and throughout most of California's share of the Peninsular Ranges, this granitic rock is now well exposed. In the northern Santa Anas, however, its distribution is less extensive. The highest peaks in the range, Santiago and Modjeska peaks (together called Old Saddleback), are still covered by the older, overlying metamorphic rocks.

The granitic rocks are still rising today, more than offsetting the leveling effects of erosion. Thus, although the rocks of the Santa Ana Mountains range between old and ancient, the origin of the range itself as a structural unit is quite recent.

Of more than casual interest to Orange Countians is the fact that for at least the past 10 million years, the Peninsular Ranges province (along with the present Los Angeles Basin and a wedge of coastal central California) has been drifting northwest relative to the rest of the North American continent. In a global view, this motion is seen as a lateral sliding (or rather a repeated lurching) at the interface between the largely oceanic Pacific Plate and the largely continental North American Plate. The average rate of movement today is about 2 inches per year—enough, if it continues, to put Orange County abreast of San Francisco 12 million years from now.

The famous San Andreas Fault (which passes about 40 miles northeast of Orange County) is the principal division between the two plates. But earth movement can also take place along "splinter" faults south and west of the San Andreas. One such splinter fault, the Elsinore Fault, passes along the eastern base of the Santa Ana Mountains. Horizontal and vertical movements along this fault over the past 5 million years have shifted the Santa Ana Mountains northwest relative to the adjacent landforms to the east, and have raised and tilted the whole mountain block into the characteristic west-sloping orientation. Sudden earth movements along any of these faults have been and will again be responsible for most of Southern California's devastating earthquakes.

The geologic history of Orange County is a fascinating one, and the diversity of landforms and rocks in Orange County and the Santa Ana Mountains is enough to pique the curiosity of most any amateur geologist. Refer to Appendix 3 for sources of more information.

Native Gardens

About 800 different kinds of wild flowering plants are found within Orange County's 782 square miles, a remarkably large number when one considers its diminutive size among California counties.

There are two reasons for this abundance of plant species. One reason has to do with physical factors: topography, geology, soils, and climate. Countywide, the diversity of physical factors and the complex interrelationships among these factors have led to the existence of many kinds of biological habitats.

The second reason is Orange County's location between two groups of flora: a southern, drought-tolerant group, most clearly represented by various forms of cacti; and a northern group, represented by moisture-loving plants typical of California's northern and central Coast Ranges. As the climate changed, varying from cool and wet to warm and dry over the past million years or so, species from one group and then the other invaded the county. Once established, many of these species persisted in protected niches even as the climate turned unfavorable for them. Some survived unchanged; others evolved into unique forms. Some are present only in very specific habitats.

The bulk of Orange County's undeveloped land can be grouped into three general classes, which botanists often call plant communities or plant associations. In a broader sense, these are biological communities, because they include animals as well as plants. These plant communities are briefly described below.

The *sage-scrub* (or coastal sage-scrub) community lies mostly below 2000 feet elevation, and extends east from the coastline to the foothills and lower spurs of the Santa Ana Mountains. The dominant species are small shrubs, typically California sagebrush, black sage, white sage, and wild buckwheat. Two larger shrubs often present are laurel sumac and lemonade berry, which like poison oak are members of the sumac family. Interspersed among the somewhat loosely distributed shrubs is a variety of grasses and wildflowers, green and colorful during the rainy season, but dry and withered during the summer and early fall drought.

The *chaparral* community is commonly found above 2000 feet elevation in the Santa Ana Mountains, where it cloaks the slopes like a thick-pile carpet. The dominant plants are chamise, scrub oak, manzanita, mountain mahogany, toyon, and various forms of ceanothus ("wild lilac"). These are tough, intricately branched shrubs with deep root systems that ensure survival during the long, hot summers. Chaparral is sometimes referred to as an "elfin forest" and that's a literal description of a mature stand. Without the benefit of a trail, travel through mature chaparral, which is typically 10–15 feet high, is

Oak woodland

almost impossible. Sage-scrub and chaparral vegetation tend to intermix readily throughout the Santa Anas, the chaparral preferring shadier, north-facing slopes, and the sage-scrub preferring hot, dry, south-facing slopes.

The *southern oak woodland* community is found in scattered locations throughout the county, from the bigger coastal canyons in the San Joaquin Hills to moist flats and canyons throughout the Santa Ana Mountains. Within the Orange County area, the indicator tree is the live oak, but sycamores may also be abundantly present. In the Chino Hills, native walnut trees form a major component of the southern oak woodland community. Beneath the trees themselves, various chaparral and sage-scrub plants often form a sparse understory.

Aside from these three widespread natural communities, much of the nonurbanized land in and around Orange County is given over to agriculture and grazing. In areas characterized by heavy grazing, one finds grassy flats and bald slopes called *potreros* (pastures) supporting mostly nonnative grasses and herbs like wild oats, filaree, mustard, and fennel.

Several other natural communities of small extent are found in Orange County: *rocky shore, coastal strand, coastal salt marsh, freshwater marsh, riparian woodland, and coniferous forest.*

The riparian (streamside) woodland community, existing in discontinuous strips along some of the bigger watercourses, is perhaps the most biologically valuable. Not only is this kind of environment essential for the continued survival of many kinds of birds and animals; it is also very appealing to the senses. Massive sycamores, cottonwoods, and live oaks, and a screen of water-hugging willows are the hallmarks of the riparian woodland. Most of this habitat has already been usurped by urbanization and by the development of water resources.

The coniferous (cone-bearing tree) forest community was once more widespread in the Santa Ana Mountains. The west-side canyons were logged a century ago in connection with various short-lived mining booms; this logging and subsequent wildfires have reduced the forest to small, isolated patches that cling to the slopes of the deeper canyons. Bigcone Douglas-fir and Coulter pine are the indicator species of coniferous forest in the Santa Anas, although live oaks and other broadleaf trees are also frequently present.

A few species of plants of limited geographic extent in Orange County are worth noting:

Knobcone pine, somewhat widely distributed in the northern and central California Coast Ranges and the foothills of the Sierra Nevada, clings to a small toehold in the Santa Ana Mountains on the slopes of Pleasants Peak. Here it finds the warm, dry climate and the particular kind of soil—serpentine—it thrives on.

California bay (bay laurel), and madrone found in the west-side canyons of the Santa Ana Mountains, are two more examples of trees at or close to the southern end of their natural range. The madrones are restricted to a tiny area in upper Trabuco Canyon.

The Tecate cypress, once widespread throughout southern California, is now confined to small "arboreal islands" in San Diego County, in northern Baja California, and along the slopes of Coal and Gypsum canyons in the northern Santa Anas (just outside the Cleveland Forest boundary). Here it finds the extra moisture, in the form of nocturnal fogs moving in from the coast, it needs in order to cling to its biological niche.

Late winter to mid-spring is the best time to appreciate the cornucopia of Orange County's native plants. Many of the showiest species—the annual wildflowers—burgeon at this time, and other plants exhibit fresh, new growth. For more information about the wildflowers, shrubs, trees, and other flora typically found in Orange County, see Appendix 3.

Creatures Great and Small

One's first sighting of an eagle, a mountain lion, a badger, or any other seldom-seen form of wildlife is always a memorable experience. Because of the diversity of the still-natural parts of Orange County, they are host to a healthy population of indigenous creatures, including a few rare and endangered species. If you're willing to stretch your legs a bit and spend some time in the areas favored by wild animals, you'll eventually be rewarded by some kind of close visual contact.

While doing field work for this book, I was lucky enough to spot a young mountain lion while hiking in the Santa Ana Mountains, and a golden eagle while driving on Interstate 5 through the hills of south county.

The most numerous large creature in Orange County is the mule deer, with a population of perhaps several hundred. These deer prefer areas of forest and chaparral, especially at higher elevations in the Santa Anas, but they can also be seen in the coastal hills and canyons, including the semi-urbanized areas around Upper Newport Bay.

The mountain lion, once hunted to near-extinction in California, has made a comeback as a protected species. Perhaps two dozen lions now roam the remote canyons of the Santa Ana Mountains and foothill areas. Counting is difficult, since mountain lions have a large territorial range (up to 100 square miles) and are normally very secretive. Because of their wide-ranging travels, however, tracks and other signs of the mountain lion are quite frequently seen.

The county's mammals also include the coyote, which has adapted to a broad range of habitats, including the margins of suburbia; the bobcat, a creature sometimes mistaken for a mountain lion, but smaller and more common; the gray fox; the skunk; the opossum; the raccoon; the ringtail cat; the badger; and various rabbits, squirrels, bats, woodrats, and mice.

Among the more commonly seen reptiles are rattlesnakes, which I will discuss in the next section.

The richness of bird life in the Orange County area is impressive, not only because of the diversity of its habitats, but also because the county lies along the Pacific Flyway route of spring-fall bird migration and serves as a wintering area for waterfowl. Several species of rare or endangered birds nest or visit, including the southern bald eagle, the peregrine falcon, the lightfooted clapper rail, the least tern, the Belding's savannah sparrow, and the least Bell's vireo.

Snowy egret

Health, Safety and Courtesy

Good preparation is always important for any kind of recreational pursuit. Hiking Southern California's backcountry is no exception. Although most of our local environments are seldom hostile or dangerous to life and limb, there are some pitfalls to be aware of.

Preparation and Equipment

An obvious safety requirement is being in good health. Some degree of physical conditioning is always desirable, even for those trips in this book designated as easy or moderate (rated ★ and ★★ in difficulty). The more challenging trips (rated ★★★ and ★★★★) require stamina and occasionally some technical expertise. Fast walking, running, bicycling, swimming, aerobic dancing, and any similar exercise that develops both the leg muscles and the aerobic capacity of the whole body are recommended as preparatory exercise.

For long trips over rough trails or cross-country terrain (there are several of these in this book) there is no really adequate way to prepare other than practicing the activity itself. Start with easy- or moderate-length trips first to accustom the leg muscles to the peculiar stresses involved in walking over uneven terrain and scrambling over boulders, and to acquire a good sense of balance. As I will note later, hiking boots rather than lightweight shoes are preferred for such travel, primarily from a safety standpoint.

Since all hiking in the Orange County area is below 6000 feet elevation, health complications due to high altitude are rare. You may, however, notice some loss of energy and more rapid breathing in the higher parts of the Santa Ana Mountains.

An important aspect of preparation is the choice of equipment and supplies. The essentials you should carry with you at all times into the backcountry are the items that would allow you to survive, in a reasonably comfortable manner, one or two unscheduled nights out on the trail. It's important to note that no one ever plans these nights! No one plans to get lost, injured, stuck, or pinned down by the weather. Always do a "what if" analysis for a worst-case scenario, and plan accordingly. These essential items are your safety net; keep them with you on all your hikes.

Chief among the essential items is *warm clothing*. Away from the coast, winter temperatures can plummet from warm at midday to subfreezing at night. Layer your clothing: it is better to take along two or more middleweight outer garments than rely on a single heavy or bulky jacket to keep you comfortable at all times. Add to this a cap, gloves, and a waterproof or water-resistant shell (a large trash bag with a hole for your head will do in a pinch) and you'll be quite prepared for all but the most severe weather experienced in the areas described in this book.

In hot, sunny weather, sun-shielding clothing is another "essential." This would normally include a sun hat and a light-colored, long-sleeved top.

Water, and to a lesser extent *food,* are next in importance. If potable water isn't immediately available, carry a generous supply. On a hot summer's day in the Santa Anas, you might need to drink up to a gallon of water on a 10-mile hike. Food is needed to stave off hunger and keep energy stores up, but it is not as essential as water in a survival situation.

Down the list further, but still "essential," are a *map* and *compass; flashlight; fire-starting devices* (examples: waterproof matches or lighter, and candle); and *first-aid kit.*

Items not always essential, but potentially very useful and convenient, are sunglasses, pocket knife, whistle (or other signaling device), sunscreen, and toilet paper.

The essential items mentioned above should be carried by every member of a hiking party, because individuals or splinter groups may end up separating from the party for one reason or another. If you plan to hike solo in the backcountry, being well-equipped is all-important. Be sure to check in with a park ranger or leave your itinerary with some other responsible person. In that way, if you do get stuck, help will probably come to the right place—eventually.

Special Hazards

Other than getting lost or pinned down by a rare sudden storm, the three most common hazards in the foothill and mountain areas are poison oak, ticks, and rattlesnakes. Poison oak, in bush or vine form, is common along many hillsides and canyons below 5000 feet. It often grows thickly on the banks of streamcourses, where it seems to prefer the semi-shade of live and scrub oaks. Learn to recognize its distinctive three-leafed structure, and avoid touching it with skin or clothing. Poison oak is deciduous, losing its leaves usually in summer or fall, but the bare

Poison oak—learn it well!

stems are no guarantee of safety: the stems continue to harbor some of the toxic resin. If there's no avoiding contact with the poison oak plant, thick pants, such as jeans, and a long-sleeved shirt will serve as fair barriers for protecting your skin. Remove these clothes as soon as the hike is over, and make sure they are washed carefully afterward. Take a bath or shower as soon as possible.

Ticks can sometimes be the scourge of overgrown trails in the Santa Ana Mountains, particularly in mid-spring when they climb to the tips of shrub branches and lie in wait for warm-blooded hosts. Ticks are especially abundant along trails used by cattle, deer, and coyotes. If you can't avoid brushing against vegetation along the trail, be sure to check for ticks frequently. Upon finding a host, a tick will usually crawl upward some distance in search of a protected spot, where it will try to attach itself. If you're aware of the slightest irritation on your body, you'll be able to intercept the tick long before it attempts to bite.

Rattlesnakes are fairly common in brushy, rocky and streamside habitats from coast to mountains. Seldom seen in either cold or very hot weather, they favor temperatures in the 75–90° range. Expect to see (or hear) rattlesnakes out and about in the daytime from early spring to mid-fall, and at night in summer and early fall. Most rattlesnakes are every bit as interested in avoiding contact with you as you are with them. Watch carefully where you put your feet, and especially your hands, during rattlesnake season. In brushy or rocky areas where sight distance is short, try to make your presence known from afar. Tread with heavy footfalls, or use a stick to bang against rocks or bushes. Rattlesnakes will pick up the vibrations through their skin and will usually buzz (unmistakably) before you get too close for comfort.

Here are a few more safety tips:

Most free-flowing water should be regarded as unsafe for drinking without purification. This does not include, of course, developed water sources within campgrounds and picnic areas. Chemical (iodine or chlorine) treatment and filtering are the most convenient purification methods, but secondary in effectiveness to boiling. A bigger problem, of course, is the availability of the water itself. Many springs and watercourses in the Santa Anas are intermittent, flowing only after winter rains. Your best bet is to carry all the water you'll need on the trail.

Deer-hunting season in Cleveland National Forest occurs during mid-autumn. Although conflicts between hunters and hikers are not common, you may want to confine your explorations at that time of year to state and county parks, where hunting is prohibited.

Mountain lions do frequent the wilder corners of Orange County and have even been spotted on the edge of suburban neighborhoods. Despite recent news stories about human-mountain lion encounters, attacks on hikers by mountain lions have remained exceedingly rare. Nonetheless, the following precautions are urged for all persons entering mountain lion country:

- Hike with one or more companions.
- Keep children close at hand.
- Never run from a mountain lion. This may trigger an instinct to attack.
- Make yourself "large," face the animal, maintain eye contact with it, shout, blow a whistle, and do not act fearful. Do anything to convince the animal that you are not its prey.
- Carry a hiking stick and use it, or pitch stones or other objects at the animal if it continues to advance.

There is always some risk in leaving a vehicle unattended at a remote trailhead. Fortunately automobile vandalism and burglary are not acute problems in the areas described in this book. Report all theft and vandalism of personal property to park officials or the county sheriff, and report vandalism of public property to the appropriate park or forest agency.

Trail Courtesy

Whenever you travel the backcountry wilderness, or even a well-trodden park trail, you take on a burden of responsibility to preserve the natural environment. Aside from common-sense prohibitions against littering and vandalism, there are some less obvious guidelines every hiker should be aware of. We'll mention a few:

Never cut trail switchbacks. This practice breaks down the trail tread and hastens erosion. Improve designated trails by removing branches, rocks, or other debris if you can. Report any trail damage and misplaced or broken signs to the appropriate ranger office (Cleveland National Forest has a form for this purpose).

When backpacking, be a "no trace" camper. Camp well away from water (there are a variety of reasons for this) and leave your campsite as you found it or leave it in an even more natural condition. Because of the danger of wildfire, you cannot have open fires (campfires, barbecues) except in developed campgrounds and picnic grounds. For cooking, you can use a camp stove (with the proper permit), but only in an area cleared of flammable vegetation.

Collecting specimens of minerals, plants, animals, and historical objects without special permit or license is prohibited in state and county parks, and in the National Forest. This means common things, too, such as pine cones, wildflowers, and lizards. These should be left for all visitors to enjoy.

It is impractical to review here all the specific rules associated with the use of public lands in the Orange County area, but you, as a visitor, are responsible for knowing them. Refer to Appendix 5 for sources of information.

READ THIS

Hiking in the backcountry entails unavoidable risk that every hiker assumes and must be aware of and respect. The fact that a trail is described in this book is not a representation that it will be safe for you. Trails vary greatly in difficulty and in the degree of conditioning and agility one needs to enjoy them safely. On some hikes routes may have changed or conditions may have deteriorated since the descriptions were written. Also, trail conditions can change even from day to day, owing to weather and other factors. A trail that is safe on a dry day or for a highly conditioned, agile, properly equipped hiker may be completely unsafe for someone else or unsafe under adverse weather conditions.

You can minimize your risks on the trail by being knowledgeable, prepared and alert. There is not space in this book for a general treatise on safety in the mountains, but there are a number of good books and public courses on the subject and you should take advantage of them to increase your knowledge. Just as important, you should always be aware of your own limitations and of conditions existing when and where you are hiking. If conditions are dangerous, or if you are not prepared to deal with them safely, choose a different hike! It's better to have wasted a drive than to be the subject of a mountain rescue.

These warnings are not intended to scare you off the trails. Millions of people have safe and enjoyable hikes every year. However, one element of the beauty, freedom and excitement of the wilderness is the presence of risks that do not confront us at home. When you hike you assume those risks. They can be met safely, but only if you exercise your own independent judgment and common sense.

Using This Book

Whether you wish to use this book as a reference tool or as a guide to be read cover to cover, you should take a few minutes to read this section. Herein I explain the meaning of the special symbols and other bits of capsulized information which appear before each trip description, and also describe the way in which trips are grouped together geographically.

One way to expedite the process of finding a suitable trip, especially if you're unfamiliar with hiking opportunities in Orange County, is to turn to Appendix 1, "Best Hikes." This is a cross reference of the dozen or so most highly recommended hikes described in this book.

Each of the 72 hiking trips belongs to one of 14 "areas." Each area has its own introductory text and map. The areas are coded according to "regions" in and around Orange County. Areas B-1, B-2, B-3, etc., are in the Beaches, Bays, and Coastal Plain region. Areas F-1, F-2, etc., are in the Foothills surrounding the Santa Ana Mountains. Letter M in the area designation refers to the Santa Ana Mountains— more precisely, the Trabuco District of Cleveland National Forest, which encompasses the Santa Ana Mountains.

The key map of Orange County and vicinity (on the pages before the Preface) shows the coverage of each area map, and the Table of Contents shows the page numbers for each region, area, and trip.

The introductory text for each area includes any general information about the area's history, geology, plants and wildlife not included in the trip descriptions. Important information about possible restrictions or special requirements (wilderness permits, for example) appears here too, and you should review this material before starting on a hike in a particular area.

The beginning of each area section contains an area map. On most of these maps, more than one hiking route (trip) is plotted, the numbers in the squares corresponding to trip numbers in the text. These boxed numbers refer to the start/end points of out-and-back and loop trips. The point-to-point trips have two boxed numbers, indicating separate start and end points. For some hikes, the corresponding area map alone is complete enough and fully adequate for navigation; for other hikes, more detailed topographical or other maps are recommended. A legend for the area maps appears on page 15.

The following is an explanation of the small symbols and capsulized information appearing at the beginning of each trip description. If you are simply browsing through this book, these summaries alone can be used as a tool to eliminate from consideration hikes that are either too difficult or too trivial for your abilities or desires.

Symbols:

 Easy Terrain: roads, trails, and easy cross-country hiking

12

Moderate Terrain: cross-country boulder hopping and easy scrambling

 Difficult Terrain: nontechnical climbing required (WARNING: THESE TRIPS SHOULD BE ATTEMPTED ONLY BY SUITABLY EQUIPPED, EXPERIENCED HIKERS ADEPT AT TRAVELING OVER STEEP OR ROCKY TERRAIN REQUIRING THE USE OF THE HANDS AS WELL AS THE FEET.)

Only *one* of these three symbols appears for a given trip, indicating the general character of the terrain encountered. As the symbols suggest, light footwear (running or walking shoes) is appropriate for easy terrain, while sturdy hiking boots are recommended for more difficult terrain.

Nontechnical climbing includes everything up to Class 3 on the rock climber's scale. While ropes and climbing hardware are not required, a hiker should have a good sense of balance, and enough experience to recognize dangerous moves and situations. The safety and stability of hiking boots are especially recommended for this kind of trip. Hazards may include loose or slippery rocks and rattlesnakes (don't put your hands in places you can't see clearly).

 Bushwhacking: cross-country travel through dense brush. This symbol is included for trips requiring a substantial amount of off-trail "bushwhacking." Wear long pants and be especially alert for rattlesnakes.

Only one of these two symbols appears:

 Marked Trails/Obvious Routes

 Navigation by Map and Compass Required (WARNING: THESE TRIPS SHOULD BE ATTEMPTED ONLY BY HIKERS SKILLED IN NAVIGATION TECHNIQUES.)

Unambiguous cross-country routes up a canyon, for example, *are* included in the first category. The hiker, of course, should never be without a map in any remote area, even if there are marked trails or the route seems obvious.

 Point-to Point Route

 Out-and-Back Route

 Loop Route

Only one of these three symbols appears, reflecting the trip as described. There is some flexibility, of course, in the way in which a hiker can actually follow the trip.

 Suitable for Backpacking.

Most trips in this book are not. Although there are several roadside campgrounds in the Orange County vicinity, trail camping is not widely permitted.

 Best for Kids

These trips are especially recommended for inquisitive children. They were chosen on the basis of their safety and ease of travel (at the time they were researched by the author), and their potential for entertaining the whole family.

Capsulized Summaries:

Distance: An estimate of total distance is given. Out-and-back trips show the sum of the distances of the out and back segments.

Total Elevation Gain/Loss: This is an estimate of the sum of all the vertical gain segments and the sum of all the vertical loss segments along the total length of the route (both ways for out-and-back trips). This is often considerably more than the net difference in elevation between the high and low points of the hike.

Hiking Time: This figure is for the average hiker, and includes only the time spent in motion. It *does not* include time spent for rest stops, lunch, etc. Fast walkers can complete the routes in perhaps 30% less time, and slower hikers may take 50% longer. The hiker is assumed to be traveling with a light day pack. (IMPORTANT NOTE: Do realize that "hiking time" stated in this book is for time-in-motion only. Also, hikers carrying heavy packs could easily take nearly twice as long, especially if they are traveling under adverse weather conditions. Remember, too, that the progress made by a group as a whole is limited by pace of the slowest member or members.)

Optional/Recommended Map(s): If no recommended map is given, then either the appropriate area map in this book or the optional map listed will suffice. Most maps, whether optional or recommended, are U.S. Geological Survey 7.5-minute series topographic maps. Usually, these are the most complete and accurate maps of the physical features (if not always the cultural features) of the area you'll be traveling in. These maps are typically stocked by backpacking, outdoor sports, and map shops around the Southern California. Even the most up-to-date topo maps (usually revised by aerial survey) often omit well-established trails and other features, so it is important to compare them with the area maps given in this book. For a list of Orange County outlets that sell maps, see Appendix 5.

Best Times: Nearly all the short trips in this book are suitable year round, but some of the longer trips, especially those inland, are much more rewarding when temperatures are mild and/or water is present along the trail.

Agency: These code letters refer to the agency or office that has jurisdiction or management over the area being hiked (for example, CNF/TD means Cleveland National Forest, Trabuco District). You can contact the agency for more information. Full names, phone numbers, and some addresses (of larger agencies) are listed in Appendix 5.

Difficulty: This overall rating takes into account the length of the trip and the nature of the terrain. The following are general definitions of the four categories:

★   **Easy.** Suitable for every member of the family.

★★   **Moderate.** Suitable for all physically fit people.

★★★   **Moderately Strenuous.** Long length, substantial elevation gain, and/or difficult terrain. Suitable for experienced hikers only.

★★★★ **Strenuous.** Full day's hike (or overnight backpack) over a long and often difficult route. Suitable only for experienced hikers in excellent physical condition.

Each higher level represents more or less a doubling of the difficulty. On average, ★★ trips are twice as hard as ★ trips, ★★★ trips are twice as hard as ★★ trips, and so on.

A final note to mountain bike riders: Many, but not all trips in this book involve terrain negotiable by mountain bike. We do, in fact, recommend some trips as being particularly rewarding by that mode of travel. Be aware, however, that regulations concerning mountain bikes in the state and county parks are subject to change. Also be aware that San Mateo Canyon Wilderness (Area M-3) is closed to all vehicles, including bicycles.

MAP LEGEND

~~	Freeway	5	Start/end point with trip number
~~	Highway		
~	Secondary road	6533 ▲	Peak (elevation in feet)
~	Minor paved road	■	Point of interest
=======	Unpaved road		
- - - - -	Foot trail / abandoned road	♦	Ranger station / fire station
· · · · · · · ·	Cross-country route	▲	Campground
=====⟋	Locked gate: no trespassing		
=====⟋	Gate: hikers OK	⊼	Picnic area
~~	Drainage (canyon, creek)	✕	Mine

Beaches and Bays

Area B-1: North Coast

Between Seal Beach and Newport Beach, Orange County's coast consists of a sandy strand broken only by the inlet to Anaheim Bay and by the mouth of the channelized Santa Ana River. Tens of thousands of people flock to these beaches on warm, sunny days, while tens of thousands more live immediately back of the coastline on low-lying land that once supported extensive salt-water and fresh-water marshes. The underlying sedimentary rocks are rich in petroleum; you're constantly reminded of that by the sight of rocker pumps, refineries, and storage tanks.

Only two areas along this north stretch of coast have been set aside to protect the last vestiges of the interior wetlands. Seal Beach National Wildlife Refuge, adjacent to the U. S. Naval Weapons Station along Anaheim Bay, is closed to public entry. Bolsa Chica Ecological Reserve, 530 acres of restored and unrestored wetlands owned by the California Department of Fish and Game, is partly open to the public. Both areas, though relatively small in size, are important as landing sites for birds migrating along the Pacific Flyway.

Trip 1: Bolsa Chica Ecological Reserve

Distance	1.5 miles
Hiking Time	1 hour
Optional Map	USGS 7.5-min *Seal Beach*
Best Times	All year
Agency	BCER
Difficulty	★

The noisy coast highway and creaking oil pumps may put you off a bit, but don't let that deter you from trying this pathway around Bolsa Chica Slough. Binoculars, spotting scopes, and/or cameras are *de rigueur*, of course.

Park in the small lot opposite the main entrance to Bolsa Chica State Beach, 1.5 miles south of Warner Avenue, or 2.5 miles north of Golden West Street. (A second parking area at Warner Avenue and Pacific Coast Highway is reserved for fishermen).

From the parking lot a long, wooden bridge leads over some shallow stretches of tide water invaded by typical salt-water marsh plants: cordgrass, alkali heath, sea lavender, and pickleweed. Interpretive panels tell of two endangered species of birds that frequent this area: the least tern, which nests on two small, sandy islands nearby; and the Belding's savannah sparrow, a bird that can drink sea water, processing it with hyper-efficient kidneys.

On the far side of the bridge a path goes left atop a levee, eventually encircling a segment of the slough. On the surface and the shoreline you may spot gulls, terns, egrets, cormorants, pelicans, stilts, plovers, avocets, grebes, marsh hawks, herons, and kites. The number and diversity of birds vary with the season.

At the west end of the path, you swing around a tidegate admitting salt water to the marsh from Anaheim Bay to the north. From this juncture you can walk up to a scenic viewpoint on the lip of a nearby mesalike terrace. Gabrieleno Indians contemplated a far different scene here prior to about 200 years ago: they beheld a broad, shallow bay extending well inland, rimmed by salt- and fresh-water marshes as far as the eye could see.

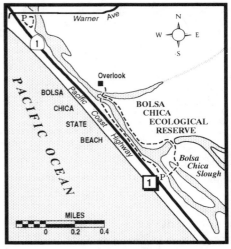

Area B-1: North Coast

Bolsa Chica Slough

Area B-2: Upper Newport Bay

The marshes surrounding Upper Newport Bay represent tiny remnants of a much more extensive wetland that once stretched inland to the present city of Tustin. The Portola expedition of 1769 and subsequent travelers passing up- or down-coast avoided this soggy region and stuck to the base of the foothills, where the firm ground more than made up for the inconvenience of traversing ridges and ravines.

During the past 100,000 years or more the Santa Ana River has wandered across the surface of the Los Angeles Basin, changing course many times in response to flooding and silt deposition. Around 30,000 years ago, the river (which at that time carried more runoff because of a wetter climate) carved out the basic form of the trough-like structure now occupied by Upper Newport Bay. Sediment carried by the river and dropped at the mouth of the trough formed a barrier island, today's Balboa Peninsula, enclosing (lower) Newport Bay.

The most recent natural shift in the Santa Ana River's course occurred in 1825, when a large flood redirected the flow west from Upper Newport Bay to essentially the place where it reaches the ocean today via artificial channel. Today the bay is fed by San Diego Creek, a small former tributary of the river.

For many millennia decayed marsh vegetation (peat) accumulated along the upper bay shores. This material, mixed with fine silt washed down from the surrounding slopes and bluffs, has created the kind of soil conditions conducive to self-sustaining wetlands.

Hemmed in by bustling traffic arteries, futuristic high-rise buildings, residential areas, and the Irvine campus of the University of California, Upper Newport Bay exists in a kind of time warp. Coyotes and mule deer still roam the periphery, while myriads of migratory birds use the productive marshes as a stopover or a winter home.

The future of the wetlands around Upper Newport Bay has been at least partly assured by the establishment of two protected areas: the Upper Newport Bay Ecological Reserve, encompassing most of the bay's salt-water marshes; and the San Joaquin Freshwater Marsh Reserve, preserving a remnant of the formerly vast inland freshwater marsh.

Trip 1: Upper Newport Bay Ecological Reserve

	Distance	1 to 2 miles
	Optional Maps	USGS 7.5-min *Newport Beach*, *Tustin*; Orange County street map
	Best Times	All year
	Agency	UNBER
	Difficulty	★

Were it not for public protest in the '60s and '70s, Upper Newport Bay would surely have become yet another of Orange County's residential harbor communities. Instead, the State of California purchased 752 acres of Irvine Company land in 1975, thus establishing the Upper Newport Bay Ecological Reserve.

An astounding 100 species of coastal and mudflat fish frequent the shallow wa-

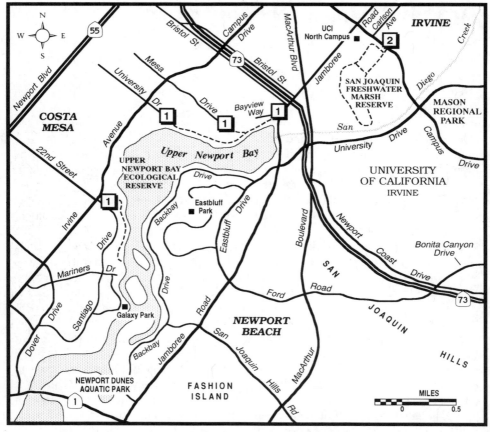

Area B-2: Upper Newport Bay

ters of the bay, as well as more than 160 species of birds. To appreciate the reserve, most people drive, bike, jog, or walk along Backbay Drive on the east shore. (Backbay Drive is one-way north for cars.) Perhaps a better approach is to meander along the many dirt paths on the north and west shores. In addition, you can follow the bayshore bikeway connecting Bayview Way with the west segment of University Drive. At one point you pass over a massively timbered wood bridge spanning the marsh where it pinches against a steep, dry bluff.

From the bridge you can view three separate tiers of vegetation. The lowest is the usual low-growing, salt-tolerant group of plants like pickleweed and cordgrass.

Just above the reach of the tide are plants typical of the coastal uplands: wild buckwheat, mule fat, cattails, plus nonnative grasses and invasive plants like castor bean, tree tobacco, pampas grass, and fennel. Above the level of the bridge, the bluff slope supports a dense growth of native coastal sage-scrub vegetation: California sagebrush, lemonade berry, elderberry, prickly pear cactus, and cholla cactus (a coastal variant of the same cactus that grows abundantly throughout southwestern U.S. deserts).

Another interesting part of the west shore can be reached from the dead end of a short residential street, Constellation Drive, off Santiago Drive, just east of the intersection of Irvine Avenue and 22nd

Street. From there a path curves down to the edge of the bay and follows the shoreline for some distance south.

From most places along the west shore there's a good view of the broad sweep of the bay's channels and marshy islands, the steep bluffs rising from the far (east) shore, and the rolling San Joaquin Hills beyond. Incised into the roughly 10-million-year-old marine sedimentary cliffs on the far side is a canyon that contained the largest assemblage of invertebrate fossils ever found in western North America.

From sea level to their highest summits, the San Joaquin Hills exhibit eight distinct marine-terrace levels. You may recognize some of these, though massive grading for construction has greatly altered the natural contour of the land. During excavation for the Fashion Island shopping center at Newport Center (cluster of high rises), a great deal of petrified wood was uncovered.

For an even broader view of the bay and surroundings, visit either Galaxy Park or Eastbluff Park in the nearby blufftop residential areas.

Path along west shore of Upper Newport Bay

Trip 2: San Joaquin Freshwater Marsh Reserve

Distance	1-2 miles
Optional Map	USGS 7.5-min *Tustin*
Best Times	October through May
Agency	SJFMR
Difficulty	★

The remnant San Joaquin Marsh owes its survival in part to its superior value for duck-hunting. In the early 1900s a private gun club made improvements to the marsh in order to make it more attractive to waterfowl. Dikes were constructed and ponds filled with water drawn from nearby San Diego Creek. Not only was the area kept off limits to potential agricultural and urban development for decades, but careful maintenance of the pond areas had a beneficial effect on nearby natural parts of the marsh

as well. In 1970, 202 acres of the duck ponds and adjacent natural areas were acquired by the University of California and incorporated into its Natural Reserve System.

Today, the restoration of degraded habitat and the return of the marsh to a state close to its original condition are two of the reserve's most important goals. Efforts are underway to remove non-native species like tamarisk and to cut back much of the vegetation that has encroached on once-open stretches of water. Because San Diego

Creek now bypasses the marsh through an artificial channel, current maintenance includes pumping groundwater up to the surface to keep the area from drying out.

The reserve is fenced and entrance is restricted, but you may join any of the guided tours given an average of twice monthly from October through May (call U.C. Irvine's Office of Natural Reserves, 949-824-6031 for information). After the tour, you may want to apply to the reserve steward for a visitor permit, which will allow you and your guests to enter the marsh and explore its paths almost anytime during the October-through-May period. Under the terms of the permit you will be expected to keep a log of your activities and report any interesting sightings of marsh fauna.

As one of the richest wetland areas remaining in Southern California, the San Joaquin Marsh offers an uncommon opportunity to come in contact with a natural ecosystem in the midst of an urban area. Concealed by screens of willows, cattails, and tules, you can spy on ducks, geese, and shorebirds and perhaps even pond turtles sunning themselves on protruding logs.

Bat houses in the Reserve

You can thrill to the graceful antics of herons and egrets, and the soaring flights of the almost ever-present marsh hawks.

Most intriguing of all, you can pay a visit to the reserve at night. Strolling down paths faintly illuminated by moonlight or sky glare, you will sense by smell, hearing, and touch and grow familiar with the damp, productive web of biological interconnection in the water, earth, and air all around you.

Upper Newport Bay

Area B-3: Crystal Cove State Park

South of Newport Bay the shoreline topography, so flat and uninspiring back along the north county coast, becomes bold and dramatic. Cliffs provide a backdrop for restless surf breaking upon smooth, sandy beaches and rocky reefs, or surging into secluded coves. In the hills behind the wavecut cliffs, you can see, imprinted on the slopes, a muted stair-step pattern of earlier cliffs that used to be ocean-fronts long before this area was uplifted to its present height.

From Corona del Mar through the posh communities of Laguna Beach and Laguna Niguel to Dana Point, rustic cottages, opulent ocean-view homes, gated housing complexes, mobile-home parks, and swank hotels blanket most of the coastline. Interspersed with these thickly populated areas lie conspicuously blank areas on the map—sensuously curved hills and lush valleys that represent what nearly all of southern Orange County was like a century ago. Fortunately, it seems, some large pieces of the undeveloped land will never succumb to the ever-rising tide of suburbia. Over the past two decades, several large parcels of undeveloped land near Laguna Beach have passed into public ownership.

Crystal Cove State Park was the first large parcel to be set aside. Besides a 3-mile stretch of bluffs and ocean front, the park reaches back into the San Joaquin Hills to encompass the entire watershed of El Moro Canyon—over 4 square miles of natural ravines, ridges, and terrace formations. In the backcountry

(El Moro Canyon) section of the park alone, visitors can explore 17 miles of dirt roads and paths open to hikers, equestrians, and mountain bicyclists. Several more miles of paved bike path and trail lace the coastal blufftops and descend to the beach.

South and west of Crystal Cove State Park, three large parcels of land in the San Joaquin Hills, owned for many decades by the Irvine Company and by other large landholding corporations, are passing into public ownership. One large section, the Aliso/Wood Canyons Regional Park, east of Laguna Beach, has gained instant popularity among both hikers and mountain bikers. The other two sections, on both

Tidepool patterns at the shore

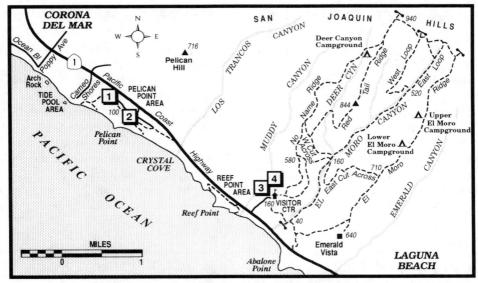

Area B-3: Crystal Cove State Park

sides of Laguna Canyon Road, have been designated Laguna Coast Regional Park. The Aliso/Wood park is described in Area B-4 of this book.

Wildfires swept nearly the whole of Crystal Cove State Park and adjoining areas around Laguna Beach in October 1993. Higher-than-average rainfall in the two years that followed has allowed much of the vegetation to return. During near-future years of heavy rainfall, you can look forward to excellent displays of wildflowers, February through April, that tend to thrive in ash-fertilized soils.

Crystal Cove State Park is open for day use from dawn to dusk. You can park along the beach and enjoy some tidepooling or beach-walking. Or you can drive up to the parking area adjoining the visitor center just east of Pacific Coast Highway, and start your exploration of the backcountry sector of the park from there. There are no drive-up campsites, but hike-in camping is permitted at the Lower El Moro, Upper El Moro, and Deer Canyon trail camping sites.

The park's interpretive program includes occasional lectures and weekly outdoor activities such as bird-watching sessions, tidepool walks, and canyon hikes. As at any California state park, expect to pay a substantial parking fee for attending events or just exploring on your own. These fees go a long way toward maintaining the park's facilities and infrastructure, which are designed to accommodate heavy use.

Trip I: **Little Corona Oceanfront Rock-hop**

Distance	1 to 2 miles
Optional Map	USGS 7.5-min *Laguna Beach*
Best Times	Low tide; October through March
Agency	CCSP
Difficulty	★

Some of the finest tide pools in Orange County—indeed in all of Southern California—await you on this short, absorbing, and probably time-consuming walk. Wear an old pair of rubber-soled shoes or boots, and expect to get wet below the ankles. In order to stay dry above there, don't turn your back to the ocean when close to the breaking waves.

Successful tidepooling—without snorkeling, at any rate—requires both good light (midafternoon is best) and minus tides. These conditions are normally satisfied near the time of either new or full moon during the period from October through March. On about 20 afternoons each year, the tide drops to less than 1 foot, which is low enough for you to examine marine life at the lowermost intertidal zone. Plan to start your walk about an hour before predicted low tide.

Rocky reefs are exposed frequently along Crystal Cove State Park's beach front, but not to the degree found along a 0.5-mile stretch of coast just north of the park. This magnificent coastline is walled off from the interior by beachfront homes in the Cameo Shores development, but you can reach it from either the northernmost parking area

in the state park's Pelican Point area, or from Little Corona City Beach, just below the intersection of Ocean Boulevard and Poppy Avenue (it may be difficult to find a place to park near Little Corona). Along this stretch, as everywhere along the California coast, beachfront private property extends only to the mean high tide line; public passage is permitted below.

From the Pelican Point parking area, a paved bike trail swings toward the bluff's edge. From here you descend to the end of a long, sandy beach, and turn up-coast over boulders and finlike rock formations into the tidepool area. The rock formations in the tidepools and the nearby cliffs are thinly bedded shales, gently tilted and locally contorted, dating back about 12 million years. In most but not all places in the intertidal zone, this rock affords good traction even when wet.

On your way up toward Little Corona Beach you'll pass two picturesque sea stacks just offshore, both pierced by wave action. The northern of the two is named Arch Rock, but either could just as well have been called Bird Rock for the ever-present pelicans and other avian life.

In the intertidal strip itself, a few

Urchins in Little Corona tidepools

dozen steps from high-tide to low-tide level encompass a complete spectrum of marine plants and animals adapted to the various degrees of inundation and exposure. In the high intertidal zone, hardy species like periwinkle snails, limpets, mussels, barnacles, and green sea anemones are found. Some of these creatures are adapted to survival in habitats moistened only by the splash of breaking waves. Shore crabs patrol these bouldered spaces, but they're likely to be hiding when you're looking for them.

Closer to the surf, the middle intertidal zone features the rock depressions called tidepools, and luxuriant growths of surfgrass, which look like bright, shiny green mats of long-bladed grass. The tidepools serve as refuges for mobile animals like fish, shrimp, and the sluglike sea hare, as well as some of the relatively immobile animals like urchins and various shellfish. Here the effects of biological erosion (or weathering) are apparent in the many pits and cubbyholes in the rocks occupied by various creatures.

In the low intertidal zone, many kinds of seaweeds thrive, including the intriguing sea palm. Animal life, however, is usually concealed beneath the rocks. Carefully pick up a rock and you may discover sea stars, sea urchins, sponges, worms, chitons, snails, abalones, and hermit crabs. If you're very lucky, an octopus may come your way. Remember that all marine life, shells, and rocks are protected; if you pick up a rock, replace it exactly where you found it, to preserve the habitat of the creatures depending upon it.

Trip 2: Crystal Cove Beaches

Distance	1 to 5 miles
Optional Map	USGS 7.5-min *Laguna Beach*
Best Times	All year
Agency	CCSP
Difficulty	★ to ★★

Hemmed in by hundred-foot cliffs on one side and the restless surf on the other, Crystal Cove State Park's 3 miles of sandy beach front seem strangely detached from the busy world above. Aside from the quaint beachfront-cottage community at Crystal Cove, recognized on the National Register of Historic Places, the midportion of the beach is largely free of encroachment by manmade structures. Come very early in the day, or anytime on a rainy day, and you'll probably have the beach all to yourself.

From any of several parking areas on the blufftops above, you can make a short loop trip along the beach and bluffs, utilizing stairs, ramps, and bike trails. Or, using a car shuttle, you might walk the entire length of beach from, say, the north end near Pelican Point to the south end near Abalone Point.

The blufftops represent the first (other than the one being cut now at beach level) of several successively higher and older marine terraces extending back into the interior San Joaquin Hills. Stay on the designated paths so as not to trample the sage-scrub plant and wildlife community that has been reestablished here. Much of this vegetation looks brown and drab in the summer and fall months, when it is dormant, but it turns green and colorful during the rainy season.

The tops of the bluffs are excellent for watching the near-shore migration of gray whales from December through February. Using binoculars, scan the ocean surface out to a distance of 1 or 2 miles. Early- to mid-morning light (sidelight) is best for this.

Below the cliffs on the gently shelving beach, you can scuff through the warm, squeaky sand above the high-tide line, tip-toe through the beached kelp along with flocks of nervous shorebirds, or cool off in the undulating wash of the surf. Swimmers and surfers should beware of the rocky reefs submerged at higher tides. During low tides, the rocky reefs are exposed, promising tidepool discoveries.

Trip 3: Emerald Vista Point

Distance	5.0 miles
Total Elevation Gain/Loss	900'/900'
Hiking Time	2½ hours
Recommended Map	USGS 7.5-min *Laguna Beach*; or Crystal Cove State Park backcountry map
Best Times	October through April
Agency	CCSP
Difficulty	★★

On the most transparent winter days, the view from Emerald Vista Point spans more than 200 miles of southern California coast and extends out to sea for a distance of 100 miles or more. Beyond Dana Point to the southeast, the low profile of San Diego's Point Loma can be traced along the curving shoreline, while offshore the diminutive Coronado Islands (just south of the international border) barely rise above the ocean haze. Southwest and west stand two big islands, San Clemente and Santa Catalina, the former a gently rising blister on the ocean surface, the latter a bold headland sprawling across 25 degrees of ocean horizon. Over the top of the upthrust Palos Verdes peninsula and through the often murky Los Angeles Basin to the northwest, you can sometimes spy the Santa Monica Mountains and the faint blue coastline reaching west toward Santa Barbara.

Morning light is best for distant views, so plan an early start. From the entrance to the visitor center parking lot, take the wide trail leading south across a grassy flat. You soon begin a short, steep descent into the flat bottom of Moro Canyon (0.4 mile), where you meet a wide, well traveled trail going up the canyon. Turn left, heading up-canyon, then very quickly turn right on a narrow trail going up a grassy slope to the south. After climbing about 200 feet, you connect with a service road wind-

Bluffs at north end of Crystal Cove

ing up the west spur of El Moro Ridge. Continue climbing up the service road for 0.7 mile, then make a sharp right on a spur leading south to a small antenna facility on the shoulder of the ridge. This is where views of Emerald Bay, the city of Laguna Beach, and the previously described distant ocean views are most panoramic.

For a longer, more leisurely descent, follow the service road farther north along El Moro Ridge, then veer left down the "East Cut-Across" road to El Moro Canyon. Turn left there and go down-canyon 1.0 mile to reach the wide trail leading out of the canyon and back toward the visitor center.

If you are backpacking, you'll be traveling farther north up El Moro Ridge. Add another 1.2 miles for the round trip to the Lower El Moro trail camp, or 2.8 miles round trip if you're heading to the Upper El Moro trail camp.

Trip 4: El Moro Canyon Loop

Distance	8.2 miles
Total Elevation Gain/Loss	1400'/1400'
Hiking Time	5 hours
Recommended Map	USGS 7.5-min *Laguna Beach*; or Crystal Cove State Park backcountry map
Best Times	October through June
Agency	CCSP
Difficulty	★★★

This is the grand tour of the Crystal Cove backcountry. During the first half you'll enjoy wide-ranging views from the spine of a prominent ridge. During the second half you'll admire some of Orange County's finest oak woodlands, tucked deep within the V-shaped fold of El Moro Canyon.

Regardless of the season, this is dry country. Fill up your water bottles at the visitor center and take along a generous supply. Be aware of the usual hazards: rattlesnakes, poison oak (in El Moro Canyon), and ticks. All three are most likely to be problems in the spring.

From the visitor center parking lot take the dirt road leading east toward a dry, scrub-covered ridge. Immediately this road splits; take the right branch, which is the more gradual and scenic of the two (the left branch proceeds directly up and over the ridge). After you climb a little along a southeast-facing slope, fine views open up of lower El Moro Canyon (called "Moro Canyon" on some maps), the surrounding hills, and the blue ocean. Hawks and ravens soar on the updrafts generated on the slopes by the morning sunshine.

After 0.8 mile a powerline road on the right drops straight down into El Moro Canyon. Stay left and you soon merge with the road branch not taken earlier. From here proceed north along the ridgeline. At the next intersection, turn right on the dirt road dubbed "West Cut-Across" and descend only 0.2 mile. Then take the road to the left; it contours around a steep ravine (Deer Canyon) then climbs to the nose of the ridge between El Moro and Deer canyons (Red Tail Ridge).

So far the foreground scenery has been marred a little by crisscrossing powerlines and by vegetation consisting largely of nonnative weedy shrubs and grasses typical of areas too heavily grazed for too long a period in the past. But as you approach the 844-foot survey point labeled "Center" on the topo map, the scenery markedly improves. Gone now are the weedy growths of mustard and artichoke thistle. The trail narrows to footpath-width and passes delicately sculpted outcrops of sandstone. The native coastal sage-scrub vegetation crowding the trailside exudes a warm, spicy odor. In spring, the colorful blooms of sticky monkeyflower, goldenbush, and paintbrush play counterpoint to the muted greens of the sages, buckwheat, laurel sumac, and lemonade berry. Interesting to examine from a safe distance are the common prickly pear cactus and the somewhat uncommon coast cholla cactus, whose easily detached bristling joints may snag the skin, clothing, or shoes of careless passersby.

At one point along Red Tail Ridge, most of the near and far suburban landscapes are temporarily veiled from sight by intervening ridges, and for a moment you can picture southern Orange County as it was about a hundred years ago. On clear days, Mount San Antonio (Old Baldy) pokes up behind a nearby ridge to the north, and Santa Catalina Island seems to float out at sea like a mountain range cast adrift from the mainland.

Up Red Tail Ridge a little farther, the trail becomes road-width again, and you can look down upon Deer Canyon trail camp nestled in a grove of sycamores in the shallow canyon to your left. A short spur trail, ahead, descends to the trail camp.

Still farther up the ridgeline, a gate across the road blocks entry into fenced, private (Irvine Company) land ahead. The new San Joaquin Hills Transportation Corridor toll road slices across the hills just north of here, bringing unaccustomed traffic noise to this formerly serene corner of

Hikers in Crystal Cove State Park

southern Orange County. About 150 yards shy of this gate, however, you pick up a narrow trail on the right leading southeast toward El Moro Canyon, parallel to the fenceline. After 0.4 mile on this trail, you join another road, entering the park from private lands to the north. Just ahead, stay left at the next junction. This puts you on the more scenic "East Loop" road into El Moro Canyon, rather than the less scenic "West Loop."

A steep (average 20 percent for 0.3 mile) grade follows, the bane of mountain bikers traveling either up or down, and hikers too. But afterward, you can let gravity repay you in a gentle way; for the next 3 miles you'll be gradually descending along the bottom of El Moro Canyon.

Upper El Moro Canyon is far and away the most beautiful attraction in the park's backcountry. You stroll past thickets of willow, toyon, elderberry, and sycamore, all brightly illuminated by the sun; then you suddenly plunge into cool, dark, cathedral-like recesses overhung by the massive limbs of live oaks. In one such recess, several shallow caves, adorned with ferns at their entrances, pock a sandstone outcrop next to the road. Prior to the establishment of the California missions, coast-dwelling Indians gathered acorns, seeds, and wild berries in this canyon. These foods, coupled with the abundant marine life nearby, provided a balanced and healthy diet.

Continue down El Moro Canyon until you approach a trailer park near the canyon's mouth. Make a right turn there and return to the visitor center.

Area B-4: Laguna Coast

The quintessentially coastal town of Laguna Beach blankets pillowy hills that rise abruptly from the sea to an elevation of nearly 1000 feet. Many of its finest houses cling precipitously to ledges cut into the steep slopes. Other houses seemingly defy gravity by resting upon cantilevered platforms or spidery networks of steel poles. There is an almost universal striving to capture a piece of the view, which without a doubt encompasses one of California's most dramatic stretches of coastline.

Much of the region's scenic beauty belongs to the public as well. Public-access paths and stairways reach down to a number of delightful pocket beaches in and near Laguna Beach, but they provide little space for walking exercise. (For sheer heart-pounding exercise, though, the precipitous stairs to Thousand Steps Beach in South Laguna can't be beat!)

Just inland from Laguna Beach, the new Aliso/Wood Canyons Regional Park spreads across lands formerly owned by private developers and formerly posted against trespassing. The park has become an instant hit with all sorts of self-propelled travelers, though mountain bikers currently predominate. There you can walk for many miles and ascend to heights furnishing truly panoramic views

West of the new park and just north of Laguna Beach, more private land is passing into public ownership to become Laguna

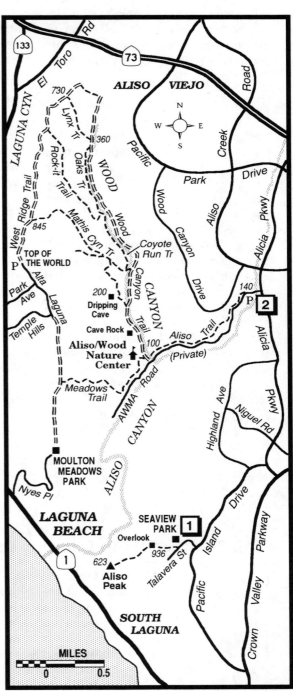

Area B-4: Laguna Coast

Coast Wilderness Park. Access to this land may be had by joining hiking, horseback riding, and mountain-biking tours led by The Nature Conservancy, which is currently charged with managing the future park (call 714-832-7478 for information and reservations).

The following two trips let you discover one of the finest overlooks along the California coast and guide you into the quiet recesses of the Aliso/Wood Canyons park.

Trip 1: Seaview Park Overlook

Distance	0.5 mile or more
Optional Map	USGS 7.5-min *San Juan Capistrano*
Best Times	All year
Agency	AWCRP
Difficulty	★

Starting from Seaview Park in the city of Laguna Niguel, this brief walk will take you past several interpretive panels annotating the common species of coastal vegetation found throughout coastal Southern California. The path leads to a concrete platform offering a jaw-dropping view of the hills of Laguna Beach spilling down to the ocean. If you live in Orange County, this somewhat obscure overlook is a good spot to keep in mind when entertaining out-of-town relatives or friends.

You start at the end of Talavera Street, off Pacific Island Drive, 1.6 miles north of Crown Valley Parkway. On some maps, the starting point is identified as Niguel Hill (936'). Start walking at the west end of the grassy strip running along the brink of Aliso Canyon. Follow a wide,

ridge-running path going west. Notice the differences between the types of vegetation growing on the two sides of the path. Dense chaparral clings to the steep, north-facing slope to the right, which drops a sheer 800 feet to Aliso Creek. A sparser assemblage of mostly coastal-sage-scrub plants lies exposed to the sun's harshest rays on the left, south-facing, side of the path.

Only a few minutes walk takes you to the concrete platform. Most casual hikers will likely want to turn back there. Beyond the platform, a narrower trail continues: it pitches sharply downward, skirts a residential street, and then rises a little to reach Aliso Peak (Aliso Summit). From there the ocean shore lies just 0.4 mile away—600 feet below.

Trip 2: Aliso/Wood Canyons Loop

Distance	10.0 miles
Total Elevation Gain/Loss	950'/950'
Hiking Time	5 hours
Optional Map	USGS 7.5-min San Juan Capistrano, *Laguna Beach*
Best Times	November through June
Agency	AWCRP
Difficulty	★★★

Aliso/Wood Canyons Regional Park consists of 3879 acres of shallow canyons, sandstone rock formations, narrow strips of oak and riparian woodland, and hillsides draped with aromatic sage-scrub vegetation. Subdivisions and subdivisions-in-the-making press in along the park's boundary and split the park into two major branches—a very narrow strip following Aliso Canyon (Aliso Creek) northeast through suburbia, and a broader stripe following secluded Wood Canyon north from Aliso Canyon. There is, as yet, no public access to the south half of the park lying in lower Aliso Canyon.

Long used for sheep and cattle grazing, the park came into being (starting in 1979) when various land developers holding title to the property deeded over parts of their holdings to Orange County for the purpose of open-space preservation. They did this in exchange for the rights to develop other acreage nearby. This pattern of land development linked to land preservation will continue in southern Orange County until nearly all the existing land used for ranching or agriculture either becomes parkland or is urbanized.

This trip takes you on a grand, looping tour of the Wood Canyon section of the park. The park's multiuse trails accommodate all sorts of self-propelled travelers. You will unavoidably encounter passing mountain bikes, though our route does try to avoid the trails most favored by mountain bikers. I recommend that you try to explore the park during the gorgeous "green" months of February through April. During the summer, the midday hours are uncomfortably warm, though the early morning and pre-sunset periods are often fairly cool. The park is open daily, 7 a.m. to sunset.

Start at the park's primary trailhead, a large parking lot alongside the AMWA (Aliso Water Management Agency) Road, just west of Alicia Parkway in the city of Laguna Niguel. The first part of the hike is, frankly, unexciting, though it is flat and easy. You follow the shoulder of the private AWMA access road for about 0.7 mile, then diverge on a trail that stays within a short distance of the road. The glimpses you get of sandstone outcrops on hillsides to the north are intriguing. This sandstone was derived from layers of sand deposited in an offshore environment some 15 million years ago. Soon you will see a lot more of this sandstone at close range.

At 1.4 miles you arrive at the park's tiny nature center/ranger station, which stands where the two canyons—Aliso and Wood—join. Picnic benches and restrooms are here. Head north on Wood Canyon Trail (the dirt road up Wood Canyon) and you soon spy, on the left, Cave Rock, a series of "wind caves" pocking a sandstone ledge. When weak sedimentary rock such as this is exposed to air and dripping water, the effects of chemical weathering loosen the mineral grains which are cemented together in the rock. Winds then scour out hollows such as you see here.

Continue north on the Wood Canyon Trail until, at 2.2 miles, you find and follow the side trail on the left leading to Dripping Cave. This impressive overhang, tucked into a narrow ravine, was the supposed hideout of 19th Century stagecoach and livestock thieves. Holes bored into the cave's walls once held pegs used to hang supplies, and the black color of the cave's ceiling is evidence of past campfires. Ferns cling to the ledge above the cave, nourished by dripping water during much of the year.

Retrace your steps for a few paces and veer left on the narrow trail—for hikers only—going northwest. You contour across a steep hillside, pass some elaborately sculpted sandstone formations on the far side of a ravine, and drop precariously onto the flat floor of shallow Mathis Canyon. Turn left on the Mathis Canyon

Trail and stay right at the next split. A 500-foot, no-nonsense climb atop a narrow ridge ensues. This may be eased by the pauses you take to admire the ever-widening views of Wood Canyon—an island of green or gold amid an endless suburban tapestry spreading inland. Hawks, ravens, and vultures patrol the air space around you, gliding by at close range or spiraling upward on thermals.

At 3.8 miles, the sweaty ascent ends as you reach the West Ridge Trail, a wide, graded fire road coming down from "Top of the World" in the city of Laguna Beach. Turn right (north) and enjoy fine views of the sharp gash of Laguna Canyon to the left and the more gentle watershed of Wood Canyon on the right. At 5.2 miles, find and follow the narrow Lynx Trail on the right (very steep in a couple of spots) down a ridge and into upper Wood Can-

yon. On this trail the viewshed is pristine—no sign of anything other than precipitous hillsides clothed in dense chaparral and live oaks. The breeze blowing up the canyon often bears the scent of marine air tinged with sage.

At the bottom of the Lynx Trail, turn right on the Wood Canyon Trail. Close ahead, veer right on the Oaks Trail, a parallel trail down the canyon which bears less mountain-bike traffic than the Wood Canyon Trail. Following a narrow strip of oak woodland along the Oaks Trail, and later the Coyote Run Trail, you reach—after nearly 2 miles of travel in shady Wood Canyon—Mathis Canyon Trail. Veer left to cross Wood Canyon's tiny creek and to hook up with the Wood Canyon Trail again. Continue south to the nature center, and from there return to the Alicia Parkway trailhead the way you came.

Mustard in bloom on coastal bluffs

Area B-5: South Coast

Life seems to pass a little more slowly along Orange County's southernmost stretch of coastline. Relatively far removed from oil pumps, snarling traffic and the crush of people upcoast, the narrow beaches and eroded cliffs are quite in tune with the rhythm of the surf and the tides. While San Clemente may have its share of elegant houses and condominium complexes spilling over the coastal bluffs and foothills, it still boasts several miles of tranquil beach nearby. Away from the main focal points of activity, such as San Clemente Pier, you can still enjoy a warm evening's stroll on the sand with no other than shorebirds as companions.

In this section, I'll elaborate on the two best beach walks south of Dana Point. One of them, San Onofre State Beach, is just over the line in San Diego County. I've included it because it is readily accessible to Orange Countians.

Trip 1: San Clemente State Beach

Distance	3 miles
Total Elevation Gain/Loss	150'/150'
Hiking Time	1½ hours
Optional Map	USGS 7.5-min *San Clemente*
Best Times	All year
Agency	SCSB
Difficulty	★

From Dana Point to San Mateo Point, a long, gently curving stretch of sand and surf beckons surfers, swimmers, sunbathers and strollers. In the north half, both the old coast highway and the tracks of the Santa Fe Railroad follow the beach. South into San Clemente, the highway turns inland, while the tracks, chiseled along the base of tan-colored cliffs, continue near the tideline.

South of San Clemente State Beach, the coastline is scenic and isolated, and it receives few visitors—good reasons why ex-President Richard Nixon located his "Western White House" here. Only the sudden thunder of a passing train, every hour or so, disturbs the beachgoer's reverie of curling breakers, shifting sands, and salt-laden breezes.

On the loop route described here you begin by walking on the beach, but return via an inland route that skirts the mouth of San Mateo Creek. The starting point is San Clemente State Beach, off Avenida Calafia, west of Interstate 5. This camping/picnic area on the bluff overlooking the beach has a large day-use parking area (fee charged). Parking is also available in the residential areas outside the entrance, or across Interstate 5 on Avenida San Luis Rey.

From the day-use area, descend to the beach on either of the two trails that drop 120 feet through gaps in the cliff wall. The cliffs, consisting of marine deposits about 15 million years old, form the blunt edge of the marine terrace on which much of the city of San Clemente rests. Today, the forces of erosion, including the not-insignificant pitter-patter of countless bare feet down the paths and the chiseling of inscriptions in the rock, help to loosen sand grains and hasten their return to the sea.

Cross the tracks through an underpass and head south along the beach onto a posted stretch overlooked by a row of modern homes. Although the upper beach is private here, California law protects public use and passage below the mean-high-tide line.

Tall palms and cypress trees on the left conceal most of the former Western White House, but a round structure—the "Card Room," where Nixon and Dwight Eisenhower used to enjoy card games—is perched on the cliff edge.

The cliffs peter out at San Mateo Point, where Orange County ends and San Diego County begins. In the water gap just ahead lies the marshy mouth of San Mateo Creek. On the right is Trestles Beach (part of San Onofre State Beach), a favorite of surfers. Ahead a little and back of the white sand lies a shallow, cattail-fringed pond where San Mateo Creek comes to an inglorious end after winding more than 20 miles from the southern Santa Ana and Santa Margarita mountains. Only during wet periods does the flow of water breach the sand to reach the ocean. This a good place to watch migratory birds, especially in winter.

Head inland now by crossing under the low railroad trestle that gave the beach its name. Pick up a paved service road/bike path, often clogged with surfers portaging their boards. After 0.3 mile, you'll reach the main bicycle path paralleling Interstate 5 through Camp Pendleton. Turn left (north) here and after 0.2 mile you'll come up to Avenida del Presidente, the west frontage road of I-5. Follow Avenida del Presidente another 0.8 mile north to Avenida San Luis Rey, where a pedestrian pass-through on the left leads into the fenced state campground.

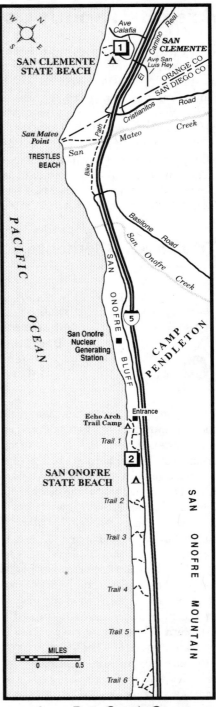

Area B-5: South Coast

Trip 2: San Onofre State Beach

Distance	1 to 6 miles
Optional Map	USGS 7.5-min *San Onofre Bluff*
Best Times	All year
Agency	SOSB
Difficulty	★ to ★★

San Onofre State Beach is perhaps best known as a busy camping spot midway between the Los Angeles and San Diego metropolitan areas. More than 300 campsites (including 40 primitive sites at Echo Arch campground) serve the needs of traveling motorists, bicyclists, and (rarely) backpackers headed up or down the coast.

The state beach includes two parcels of land leased from the Marine Corps, whose big Camp Pendleton base sprawls for 17 miles down the coast from San Clemente. The northern section extends from the Orange County line (Trestles Beach) to the San Onofre Nuclear Generating Station. The second, more easily reached section includes about 3 miles of ocean frontage south of the power plant.

To reach the state beach entrance, take the Basilone Road exit from Interstate 5, turn west, and follow the westside frontage road—the old Highway 101—downcoast 3 miles (you pay a parking fee here). In the next 3 miles, the old roadbed is partitioned into camping spaces for campers and trailers, and day-use parking areas. Day users can park in the large lots in the first and last half-miles, or in areas designated for day use on the roadbed's east side.

It's worth taking at least a brief look at the sage-scrub vegetation on top of the bluffs. These are fairly dense and undisturbed stands, accented with taller shrubs like laurel sumac, lemonade berry, toyon, and tree tobacco. Red and sticky monkeyflower plants are here, producing

The beach at San Clemente

a variety of colors during the spring bloom: red, orange, salmon pink, and yellow. The red variety is a great attractor of hummingbirds. Bladderpod, a familiar plant of California's deserts, also makes a home among the sage scrub here.

A total of eight dirt roads and paths descend through ravines or breaks in the bluff wall to reach the white-sand beach below. There the sounds and sights of civilization are gone, and you're left to explore a primeval stretch of coastline. Strolling along the water's edge, you may spot dolphins, sea lions, and harbor seals. My companions and I once watched a pair of dolphins cavorting in the surf less than 50 feet from the shore. Some secluded spots in the southern reaches of the state beach are used by nudists—though not legally.

In the northern reaches of the state beach, near Echo Arch campground, the eroded cliff faces are especially interesting and photogenic. Some are reminiscent of the naturally sculpted stone formations in Utah's Bryce Canyon National Park. The campground rests on old landslide debris that spalled off the concave cliff face that partly surrounds the campground. This sliding or slumping process repeats itself many times over geologic time—though usually on a less dramatic scale—as the ocean waves nibble at the bluffs and undercut them.

Try exploring the stretch of beach just north of Echo Arch while keeping a sharp eye on the strata exposed on the face of the sea bluff there. You'll discover the Cristianitos Fault, a crack in the earth that extends some 25 miles inland. To the right (south) side of the fault's inclined surface you'll see the brownish Monterey shale, a fine-grained sedimentary rock deposited some 15-20 million years ago. To the left of the fault is the off-white San Mateo sandstone, laid down an estimated 5 million years ago. Above both of these formations lies a flat layer of boulders deposited in a marine environment about 120,000 years ago, and other land-laid deposits on top of the bouldery layer. The undisturbed nature of these upper layers has assured geologists that the Cristianitos Fault has been moribund for at least 120,000 years and therefore is almost certainly not a threat to the stability and safety of the nuclear power plant, which is located less than a mile up the coast. Other faults, however, are known to exist several miles to the southwest. These offshore faults are thought to be extensions of faults exposed on land that are known to have been active in historic times.

Eroded cliffs, San Onofre State Beach

Foothills

Area F-1: Chino Hills

Seen from the air, the Chino Hills look like a rumpled bedsheet tossed near the northern brow of the higher Santa Ana Mountains. If they weren't cleanly separated from the Santa Anas by the broad trench of Santa Ana Canyon, these hills and their extensions to the north, the Puente Hills, would certainly be considered the northernmost expressions of the Peninsular Ranges.

Rapidly eroding, yet exhibiting a rather graceful, rounded topography, the Chino Hills consist of 5- to 15-million-year-old marine sedimentary rocks uplifted fairly recently by movements along the Whittier fault zone to the west and along lesser faults to the east. The maximum thickness of these sediments—called the Puente Formation—in the Chino Hills is 13,000 feet.

For the past two centuries the rolling, grassy swells and wooded ravines of the Chino Hills have been used for cattle and sheep grazing. Originally they were a part of lands assigned to Mission San Gabriel; later they were incorporated into various Spanish land grants or reserved as lands in the public domain. Private ranching interests acquired most of the land by the mid-20th Century. By the 1970s, however, ranching was in decline everywhere around Southern California and tract houses began popping up like mushrooms around the base of the hills. The setting aside of open space and parkland suddenly became an urgent priority.

In 1975 Orange County established the 124-acre Carbon Canyon Regional Park on the west edge of the Chino Hills. Following suit, the State of California in 1977 began a feasibility study for a large park in the Chino Hills. In 1981 the state acquired its first parcel, and by 1983 Chino Hills State Park was opened to the public. Today, after the expenditure of over $50 million (the largest sum spent on any California state park), 13,000 acres of state parkland stretch from Carbon Canyon Regional Park to the eastern edge of the Chino Hills in San Bernardino and Riverside counties. The park remains almost entirely undeveloped today, containing just one small drive-in campground, an equestrian staging area, and scattered picnic tables and privies. Future improvements may include several large-capacity drive-in campgrounds, and a half-dozen trail camps for overnight travelers.

Aside from its recreational potential, Chino Hills State Park contains important plant and wildlife habitats. About 10 percent of the park's land area is classified as southern oak woodland, a plant community that has been greatly affected by California's population explosion. Some of the best remaining stands of the California walnut, a tree whose native range is confined to the Los Angeles Basin and surrounding foothills, are found in the larger canyons of the park.

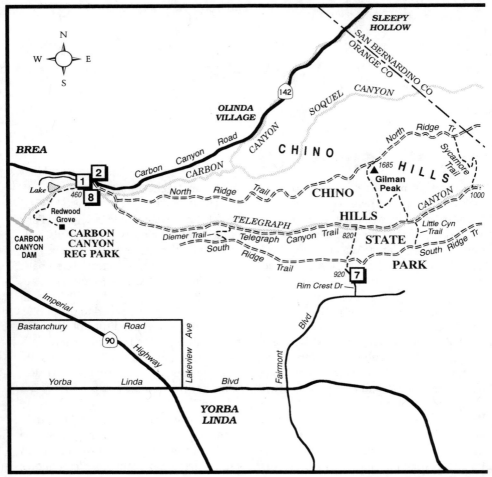

Area F-1: Chino Hills

Wildlife includes mule deer, foxes, rabbits, coyotes, bobcats, badgers, and rattlesnakes. Several rare or endangered species of birds may visit the park, including the southern bald eagle, peregrine falcon, and least Bell's vireo.

Chino Hills State Park has become popular with hikers, equestrians, and especially mountain bicyclists, all of whom who enjoy the park's primitive character. Dirt roads and old cowpaths lace the open ridgelines and thread through the shady canyons. Some 55 miles of dirt roads and trails are open to mountain bikers as well as hikers and horse riders. Certain "single

track" (narrower) trails may be closed to cyclists or cyclists and equestrians. Trail signs and the allowed uses of the trails are now posted throughout the park, and an improved trail map available on entry into the park makes navigation relatively easy. The major trails and old roads feature mile posts stating the distance (by way of the most direct route) from the park office.

Carbon Canyon Regional Park, on the east fringe of the city of Brea, boasts only one short hiking trail. Access to the Chino Hills State Park trail system on this western side is provided by the so-called Lemon Grove entry, just east of the regional park.

To Soquel Canyon Parkway

ALISO
RAPTOR CANYON
BANE CANYON
CYN
SLAUGHTER CANYON

Aliso Canyon
Trail

850

Hills for
Everyone
Trail

1330

Raptor Ridge

McDermont
Trail

4

Park Office

McDermont
Spring

730

Telegraph Canyon Trail

8 **5**

3

760

South

Ridge

Trail

1318

1040
OVERLOOK

6

P

TELEGRAPH
CANYON

1781

WATER

CANYON

Campground

**San Juan
Hill**

1040

675

Lower Aliso
Canyon Trail

Bobcat

Ridge

Trail

**CHINO
HILLS
STATE
PARK**

SAN BERNARDINO CO

ORANGE CO

BRUSH

CANYON

ALISO

CANYON

Scully

Ridge

Brush Cyn Trail

Trail

Scully Hill
Trail

MILES

0   1

SANTA   ANA   CANYON

Someday visitors will drive into Chino Hills State Park via a future road cutting through Slaughter Canyon to the east. Now and probably for some years to come, however, the park has an awkward "temporary" main entrance. From the Riverside Freeway (Highway 91) drive north on Highway 71 seven miles to the Soquel Canyon Parkway exit. From the Pomona Freeway (Highway 60) drive south on Highway 71 five miles south to the same exit. Head west on Soquel Canyon Parkway 1.0 mile to Elinvar Drive. Turn left, left again after 0.2 mile, and then immediately right on the gravel road signed CHINO HILLS STATE PARK. The semi-rough road ahead is open during park hours, 8 A.M. to sunset. After 2 miles the road becomes paved and bends sharply right. There's an equestrian staging area on a knoll to the right, and a kiosk on the left, where you can pay day-use or camping fees.

For the following trip descriptions, I've selected several shorter hikes in the Chino Hills area, plus a half-day-long stroll across the entire east-west dimension of the state park. The map of the Chino Hills appearing in this book shows the major trails of the state park and omits some unmaintained trails that receive little or no use. In recent years, some of these lesser trails have been completely overgrown by grass or brush.

Trip 1: Carbon Canyon Nature Trail

Distance	2.0 miles
Hiking Time	1 hour (round trip)
Optional Map	USGS 7.5-min *Yorba Linda*
Best Times	All year
Agency	CCRP
Difficulty	★

An unlikely grove of coast redwood trees, nursed from seedlings and planted in 1975, lies at the end of this self-guiding nature trail. Indigenous to the California coast only as far south as Monterey County, their survival in this rather dry corner of Orange County is remarkable.

The trail begins inside Carbon Canyon Regional Park, just east of the entrance. A small fee is collected for parking. This typical suburban recreational facility features various sports facilities, picnic grounds and pedestrian/bike paths. The entire park lies within the flood zone of the Carbon Canyon flood-control dam, which someday may protect urbanized areas downstream at the expense of inundating the park. The park also happens to lie squarely within the Whittier fault zone, a major splinter of the San Andreas Fault.

From the trailhead follow the designated path through a grove of planted pines and down into the bed of Carbon Canyon. The tiny stream is flanked by a variety of water-loving plants: the native mule fat and willow, and vigorous growths of "giant reed," a naturalized exotic plant resembling bamboo. These reeds are copious consumers of water, and are considered unwelcome usurpers of the natural habitat.

After what may be a muddy creek crossing, a trail on the left leads east across a grassy terrace toward Telegraph Canyon in Chino Hills State Park. Stay right. The nature trail continues west, hugging a dry hillside on the left and dense riparian vegetation on the right. A few graceful native walnut trees and non-native pepper trees can be seen along the hillside, but mostly there are rampant growths of exotic weedy plants like fennel, mustard, and castor bean. The trail briefly tunnels under a dark archway of giant reeds, then bends left into an arm of the basin just above Carbon Canyon dam. Here you find the curious stand of redwoods, a picnic bench, and a drinking fountain. Subsurface water in the basin may keep these redwoods alive, but without the rain and fog drip they are accustomed to in their native habitat, they look a bit thin and dusty.

Trip 2: Gilman Peak

Distance	7.0 miles
Total Elevation Gain/Loss	1400'/1400'
Hiking Time	3½ hours (round trip)
Optional Map	USGS 7.5-min *Yorba Linda*
Best Times	October through June
Agency	CHSP
Difficulty	★★★

View of citrus orchards from North Ridge Trail

Gilman Peak's bald summit, barely poking over lesser ridges, affords a breathtakingly spacious view of Southern California on a clear day. To the southwest lies the wide mouth of Santa Ana Canyon, scored by a broad flood channel carrying runoff that originates far inland amid the San Bernardino Mountains. Beyond, the vast urban plain of Orange County, resting on a vast sheet of alluvium, slopes gently toward the ocean. Northward, the gaunt San Gabriel Mountains, snow-capped in winter, rise boldly over foreground hills and valleys. In the southeast, the Santa Ana Mountains form a broad, dusky blister on the horizon.

One popular approach to Gilman Peak starts from the west side, at Carbon Canyon Regional Park, or just east of there. Customarily, many users of the Chino Hills trail system park their cars on the south shoulder of Highway 142 (Carbon Canyon Road), just east of the entrance to Carbon Canyon Regional Park, and start hiking or riding on a dirt road slanting southeast, just below the grade of the highway.

Following this route, you skirt a citrus orchard (one of the few remaining in Orange County) and soon reach a state park bulletin board at a trail junction.

Telegraph Canyon lies ahead; you veer left and start climbing on the North Ridge Trail, a dirt road. There are many California walnut trees to be seen in the next couple of miles, their wispy branches swaying and their compound leaves shimmering in the breeze. These trees, which cling to north-facing slopes, offer welcome shade during the warmer months. They are deciduous, dropping their leaves by the late fall and regaining them in early spring.

By 2 miles into the hike, the trail is staying high on the ridgeline, which is bald save for grass and low-growing sage-scrub vegetation. After you pass over a couple of smaller bumps on the ridge, Gilman Peak appears ahead, its summit accessible by way of a wide side trail from the northeast, and another, narrower side trail from the southwest.

Gilman Peak can also be reached by way of narrow trails running north from the Rim Crest Drive trailhead in Yorba Linda. That approach is shorter, but nearly shadeless.

Trip 3: Panorama Point

Distance	1.6 miles
Total Elevation Gain/Loss	300'/300'
Hiking Time	1 hour (round trip)
Optional Map	USGS 7.5-min *Prado Dam*
Best Times	All year
Agency	CHSP
Difficulty	★

Worthwhile as an introductory hike, this short stroll takes you to a knoll overlooking about half of Chino Hills State Park's 13,000 acres. So commanding is the view that plans call for the construction of a "Panorama Point Visitor Center" on the site. On park maps, the site is now called McLean Overlook.

On entering the park by way of Bane Canyon, you will pass an entrance booth (staffed on weekends) at a road summit. After another 1.7 miles, a dirt road signed "SCENIC OVERLOOK" appears on the left (east). There are a few paved parking spaces nearby; if all are taken, you may park at the equestrian staging area atop the ridge to the right and walk down to this point. Start walking up the dirt road, ignoring a lesser-used old roadbed on the left, that heads toward Slaughter Canyon. Both roads will likely be paved when the park's permanent main entrance through Slaughter Canyon is developed.

After 0.4 mile of steep ascent, the road levels out and continues 0.4 mile far-

ther to the overlook. The view encompasses most of the Aliso Canyon drainage. You see rolling, grass-covered hills flanking a shallow valley lined with tall sycamores. In spring the green hills are tinted by the blue-purple flowers of lupine, and accented by yellow bands of blooming wild mustard. Sometime in April or May, quite abruptly, the grass turns a tawny gold. By early fall, after months of fierce sunshine and desiccating winds, it's difficult to believe these same sere hills could ever be green again.

The clayey soils of the hills are derived from bedrock consisting mainly of weak siltstones. These soils expand when wet, and are especially prone to creeping and sliding when waterlogged. You'll notice many examples of recent slumping and gullying on the slopes. Look also for evidence of much older and larger landslides. These big ones probably developed during the last Pleistocene glacial stage (10,000–20,000 years ago) when Southern California's climate was much wetter.

Trip 4: Upper Aliso Canyon

Distance	3.8 miles
Total Elevation Gain/Loss	700'/700'
Hiking Time	2 hours
Optional Map	USGS 7.5-min *Prado Dam*
Best Times	November through May
Agency	CHSP
Difficulty	★★

The uppermost reaches of Aliso Canyon and one of its tributaries, Raptor Canyon, together form one of three areas in Chino Hills State Park deemed pristine enough to be considered "primitive areas." This and the other two primitive areas, at Water Canyon and Brush Canyon, are managed to preserve their natural character and to allow park visitors the opportunity for solitude in a wilderness-like setting.

Although this hiking route only skirts the south edge of the Upper Aliso/Raptor Canyon primitive zone, you'll appreciate the fine vistas (on clear days at least) of miles of empty hill country presided over by the snow-dusted summits of the San Gabriel Mountains.

You may begin at the park office, where abundant parking space is available. Head north past outlying staff residences and continue on an old dirt road up the west bank of sycamore-lined Aliso Canyon. At 0.7 mile, the old road passes under some high-voltage wires and soon bends decidedly west up along the bottom of a shallow tributary—Raptor Canyon. A few willows and an occasional walnut tree are all that Raptor Canyon musters for display here.

At 1.1 miles, the road veers right and zigzags up the slope to the north. Stay left on the path that strikes west up a grassy ridge just south of Raptor Canyon. After crossing under another powerline, you begin a stiff climb of about 500 vertical feet, up through tall-growing grasses and mustard plants, topping out on Raptor Ridge. On the way up, you can look out over the upper reaches of Raptor Canyon, smothered in a rich, dark growth of live oak and walnut trees. True to its namesake, you'll probably notice a hawk or two cruising on updrafts in the canyon.

In upper Aliso Canyon

At 2.0 miles, atop Raptor Ridge, the trail descends a little and you meet a powerline access road. Turn left (east), walk 0.3 mile toward a complex of electric towers, and then go right on a road that drops into the wooded drainage to the south. At the bottom (2.8 miles), turn east and return to your starting point by way of the gently descending Telegraph Canyon Trail (a graded dirt road).

Trip 5: Hills for Everyone Trail

Distance	5.0 miles (to McDermont Spring)
Total Elevation Gain/Loss	700'/700'
Hiking Time	2½ hours (round trip)
Optional Map	USGS 7.5-min *Prado Dam*
Best Times	October through June
Agency	CHSP
Difficulty	★★

The Hills for Everyone Trail (actually reserved for hikers only), commemorates "Hills for Everyone," a conservation group that was instrumental in the establishment of Chino Hills State Park. The trail runs up an unnamed tributary of Aliso Canyon, beautifully shaded by live oak, walnut, sycamore, elderberry and toyon.

From the parking lot next to the park office, walk south on the paved entrance road for about 200 yards, then turn right (west) on the Telegraph Canyon Trail—a graded dirt road closed to motor traffic. After a somewhat tedious and almost flat 0.9 mile on this, look for the Hills for Everyone Trail on the right, going up along the ravine bottom (another, wider trail continues north to Raptor Ridge). Large interpretive panels accompany the trail. For the next 1.3 miles you stick close to the ravine bottom, first on its right, then on its left. During the wet season, water trickles down the bottom, nourishing a moist, dark understory of wild berry vines, ferns, nettles, watercress, and other water-loving plants. Near the top of the trail at 1318 feet, filtered sunlight illuminates wild grape vines draped among the oak trees.

At the top you come to a saddle, part of a major watershed divide. Several trails converge in this area. Raindrops falling to the west are routed down Telegraph Canyon to Carbon Canyon, while rain falling to the east goes into Aliso Canyon. Although most precipitation received in these hills is quickly absorbed by the porous soils, all of the excess eventually makes its way to the Santa Ana River.

Just west of the saddle is McDermont

On the Hills for Everyone Trail

Spring, a small stock pond filled with cattails. Nearby an old windmill groans as it pumps water into a metal tank. Most of the old stock ponds in the park have been allowed to silt up, but this one will be maintained for passing horses and for the benefit of the local wildlife. Look for frogs, pond turtles, and a host of birds in the area

hereabouts before you return the same way.

The Hills for Everyone Trail has a tendency to get quickly overgrown after wet winters. For a spell around 1994 it had virtually disappeared. If this happens again, you may opt to follow the less scenic Telegraph Canyon Trail to reach McDermont Spring.

Trip 6: Water Canyon

Distance	4+ miles
Total Elevation Gain/Loss	500'/500'
Hiking Time	2 hours (round trip)
Optional Map	USGS 7.5-min *Prado Dam*
Best Times	November through May
Agency	CHSP
Difficulty	★★

If you're searching for the single most intriguing spot in the Chino Hills, you may find it in the upper reaches of Water Canyon. Concealed in the inky depths of this steep-walled ravine, massive sycamores and oaks reach skyward, casting a perennial chill. Except for the occasional buzz of a small aircraft and the rustle of leaves in the breeze overhead, the silence and stillness are absolute.

Park at the kiosk on the entrance road above the campground, or at the equestrian staging area, and start walking from there. Head downhill into the campground, and continue south along an old road, crossing a flat terrace dotted with graceful though weedy "trees-of-heaven." Originally from China, these fast-growing ornamental trees have become naturalized throughout California.

About 0.5 mile from the campground, you dip to cross Aliso Canyon's small stream, which can be wet or dry. On the other side, you meet another road at a T-intersection. Turn right, go about 100 yards, and go right again on the narrow trail going up Water Canyon. This is one

of the few trails in the park reserved exclusively for hikers. Equestrian and bike traffic is prohibited.

Lining Water Canyon is a narrow finger of riparian willow and sycamore growth, flanked by grizzled oaks, well-proportioned walnut trees, and more trees-of-heaven. After a short mile you pass a thicket of prickly-pear cacti so dense it forms a trailside wall. The trail, which has received little maintenance of late, deteriorates shortly thereafter and is hard to follow amid the encroaching growth of seasonal grasses. Intrepid hikers can continue another half mile up along the shady canyon bottom, often knee-high in grasses, and finally reach, in the darkest heart of the canyon near its head, a silted-up water tank that once stored water for cattle herds. (Wear long pants and watch for poison oak, stinging nettles, and rattlesnakes if you do this.) The pristine little patch of wilderness in upper Water Canyon is as close to—and as far from—from modern civilization as you will find anywhere around the L.A. metropolitan area.

Trip 7: San Juan Hill

Distance	6.4 miles
Total Elevation Gain/Loss	1200'/1200'
Hiking Time	2½ hours (round trip)
Optional Maps	USGS 7.5-min *Yorba Linda, Prado Dam*
Best Times	November through May
Agency	CHSP
Difficulty	★★★

A straightforward hike to the high point of Chino Hills State Park, 1781-foot San Juan Hill, can start from either the park office or the Rim Crest Drive trailhead in Yorba Linda. The latter is a bit longer, but it starts at a point much closer to where most Orange Countians live.

From the intersection of Fairmont and Yorba Linda boulevards in Yorba Linda, drive 1.5 miles north on Fairmont to Rim Crest Drive on the left. Go a short half mile north on Rim Crest to the signed trailhead, on the right. Curbside parking is available here.

On foot, head uphill a short distance to signed South Ridge Trail (a dirt road). Turn right, heading east along the South Ridge toward San Juan Hill. For 3 miles the trail's gently curling course takes you through a near-treeless landscape. Tall grasses on both sides of the trail sway in the stiff afternoon breezes typically blowing up Santa Ana Canyon from the west. This fact is not lost on kite flyers, who sometimes practice their art here. Keep an eye out for small herds of deer, which roam this section of the park with impunity.

After just over 3 miles of general ascent, take the narrow side trail on the right leading 0.1 mile to the San Juan Hill sum-

Sycamore and wild radish in Chino Hills State Park

mit. Nearby high-voltage powerlines spoil the view to the east; in other directions, however, the vista is pristine.

Trip 8: Telegraph Canyon Traverse

Distance	8.4 miles
Total Elevation Gain/Loss	650'/900'
Hiking Time	4 hours
Optional Maps	USGS 7.5-min *Prado Dam, Yorba Linda*
Best Times	November through May
Agency	CHSP
Difficulty	★★★

Whether you are hiker, horseman, or mountain biker, more than 8 miles of superb scenery are yours to enjoy on this one-way trek over the Chino Hills. Telegraph Canyon is long enough, wild enough, and beautiful enough (especially in its upper reaches) to provide a close approximation to a true wilderness experience. Try this trip sometime on a late-autumn afternoon, after the first rains of the season, when the sun's warm rays illuminate the gold and green sycamores, and the cool breeze has a tangy, woodsy aroma.

Going east to west is slightly easier than the other way around. So set up a car shuttle (using Carbon Canyon Road), or otherwise arrange to be dropped off at the Chino Hills State Park office parking lot and to be picked up later at Carbon Canyon Regional Park.

As in Trip 5, make your way up the Telegraph Canyon Trail and the Hills for Everyone Trail to the saddle, then drop down to McDermont Spring—the headwaters of Telegraph Canyon. (Note: mountain bikes and horses are not allowed on the Hills for Everyone Trail. They must stay on the Telegraph Canyon Trail all the way to the saddle.)

Navigational matters are very simple thereafter: just stroll down the bottom of the canyon 5.4 miles until you reach the fringe of the citrus grove at the canyon's mouth. Here, veer right (northwest) toward Carbon Canyon Road. There you'll pick up a roadside path leading a short distance west to Carbon Canyon Regional Park's east parking lot.

Autumn sunlight in Water Canyon

Area F-2: Santiago Creek/Anaheim Hills

On the eastern fringes of Anaheim and the city of Orange lie several picturesque city and regional (county) parks—all within a half-hour drive of most parts of metropolitan Orange County. This is classic urban-wildland-interface country: suburban housing developments spreading into the foothills of the Santa Ana Mountains, with nothing beyond but miles of profoundly empty land.

The trips described in this section are found in the following parks: Oak Canyon Nature Center, an Anaheim city park located in that city's Anaheim Hills district; Santiago Oaks Regional Park, east of Villa Park; Weir Canyon Regional Park, an undeveloped buffer of open space just east of Anaheim Hills; Irvine Regional Park, the county's oldest park, located just east of the city of Orange; and the Peters Canyon Regional Park, between Tustin and Orange. In addition to all this, an integrated system of multiuse (hiking, biking, equestrian) trails is slowly taking form in this area and throughout southern Orange County as well. This "urban" network of city and county trails is designed to link the various regional parks and eventually will tie into the trails of Cleveland National Forest to the east.

Trip 1: Oak Canyon Nature Center

Distance	1 to 3 miles
Optional Map	USGS 7.5-min *Orange*
Best Times	All year
Agency	OCNC
Difficulty	★

This vest-pocket wilderness park, squeezed between a golf course and a reservoir on one side and a suburban housing tract on the other, offers small children plenty of room to roam on its tightly nested, 4 miles' worth of hiking trails. It's pretty hard for the little ones to get seriously lost, and the price is right—free. For adults, this is a park to savor slowly. Habitats include a trickling stream shaded by coast live oaks, and hillsides coated with chaparral and sage-scrub vegetation. Following a heavy-rainfall season, the wildflower bloom—especially that of sticky monkeyflower—can be spectacular.

The primary mission of the Oak Canyon Nature Center is education. A slew of workshops and hikes for families and individuals are offered year round. On certain summer evenings "Nature Nights"—a twilight walk followed by a presentation in the center's outdoor amphitheater—is offered. The normal hours for the center are 9 A.M. to 5 P.M. No bikes, picnicking, or pets are allowed on the trails.

To reach Oak Canyon Nature Center from the Riverside Freeway (Highway 91), exit at Imperial Highway and drive 1 mile south to Nohl Ranch Road. Turn left there and go east 2 miles to Walnut Canyon Road. Turn left and continue to the end of the road. A few steps from the parking lot will take you to a beautiful new interpretive center, nestled under spreading oaks, where you can view some exhibits and pick up a detailed trail map.

In the park itself, numerous short trails diverge from the "Main Road," which

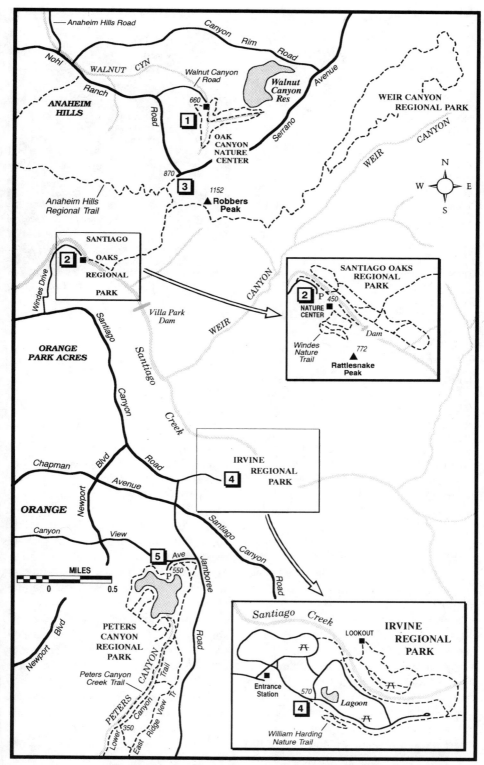

Area F-2: Santiago Creek/Anaheim Hills

is a wide path paralleling a small stream in the bottom of Oak Canyon (a tributary of Walnut Canyon). The Stream Trail meanders through the thick of the riparian and oak woodland habitats, while the Roadrunner Ridge and Bluebird trails ascend onto the steep slopes overlooking the ravine bottom. In summer, you'll find little of interest high on the shadeless, scrub-covered slopes but a lot to enjoy down amid the oaks. In spring, you'll want to gravitate toward the slopes on the south side; this is where a variety of blooming native plants stand shoulder to shoulder.

In Oak Canyon Nature Center

Trip 2: Santiago Oaks Regional Park

Distance	1 to 3 miles
Optional Map	USGS 7.5-min *Orange*
Best Times	All year
Agency	SORP
Difficulty	★

What Santiago Oaks Regional Park lacks in sheer size (250 acres) is more than adequately compensated for by its rare beauty. The core of the park is made up of two former ranch properties acquired in the mid-1970s. A small Valencia orange grove and many acres of ornamental trees planted around 1960 on these properties complement the natural riparian and oak-woodland plant communities along Santiago Creek.

As you approach the park entrance on Windes Drive, the outlying subdivisions quickly fade from sight and a lush strip of riparian vegetation—willows and sycamores—presided over by steep, scruffy slopes comes into view on the left. Beyond the entrance (day-use fee collected here) and the parking lot, you can stroll up past some oak-shaded picnic sites to the superb nature center, which is housed in a nicely refurbished 60-year-old ranch house.

About 3 miles of riding and/or hiking paths lace the park and connect with the Anaheim Hills Regional Trail described below (Trip 3). You might begin with the self-guiding Windes Nature Trail and its extension—the Pacifica Loop—starting alongside the nature center. Though only about 0.7 mile long, the trail is very steep in places; it meanders up to the northern summit of Rattlesnake Ridge, an isolated, erosion-resistant block of mostly conglomerate rock. A slice of Pacific coastline can be glimpsed from the high point of the trail, and a fenced lookout point nearby offers a view almost straight down on Santiago Creek and the rest of the park.

Back down by the nature center, you

can walk upstream along the shaded creek bank to reach a small rock-and-cement dam dating from 1892. This dam replaced an earlier one, built in 1879, that was part of one of Orange County's first irrigation systems. Today, the dam is a historical curiosity, dwarfed by the big Villa Park flood-control dam a short distance upstream, and Santiago Reservoir farther upstream.

West of the nature center, you can ford Santiago Creek and stroll along several paths amid the eucalyptus, pepper, and other exotic trees rooted in the gently sloping bench on the creek's far side. Because of the diversity of its habitats, Santiago Oaks is a delightful birding spot, with species ranging from the tree-dwelling western bluebird and acorn woodpecker to the water-loving great blue heron. On occasion, vultures and ospreys, as well as some common hawks, may be seen soaring overhead.

Trip 3: Weir Canyon Park

Distance	8.0 miles
Total Elevation Gain/Loss	2000'/2000'
Hiking Time	4½ hours
Optional Maps	USGS 7.5-min *Orange, Black Star Canyon*
Best Times	November through May
Agency	OCEMA
Difficulty	★★★

The Anaheim Hills Regional Trail skims the still-undeveloped summit ridge of the Anaheim Hills, drawing significant numbers of hikers, equestrians and mountain bicyclists. One branch of the trail plunges southward to connect with the trail system of Santiago Oaks Regional Park. Another branch meanders west along the summit ridge, following powerlines. Still another branch, described here, meanders east into the future Weir Canyon Regional Park—a patch of land earmarked for open space amid the suburbs of the future.

"Anaheim Hills" refers to a part of the Peralta Hills, an elongated ridge stretching west from the Santa Ana Mountains parallel to the lower reaches of Santa Ana Canyon. The name, not found on older maps, comes from the Anaheim Hills development, which blankets the north slopes. More housing development, and massive grading associated with it, will come eventually. Regional trails will remain, however, threading through rows of future houses on narrow corridors.

A good place to begin your exploration of the Anaheim Hills Regional Trail is the present west terminus of Serrano Avenue, which dead ends just west of Nohl Ranch Road in Anaheim Hills. If there's room, park off the pavement here; otherwise, you can find curbside parking on any nearby street. Someday, Serrano Avenue will be extended west over the hills to Villa Park, but for now you start your hike by walking west on a dirt road going down a ravine. After 0.2 mile, you join the Anaheim Hills Regional Trail—also a dirt road. Bear left and curve upward along a grassy hillside to the summit ridge another 0.2 mile ahead. Keep bearing left to follow the trail as it heads east along the summit ridge (on the right, a branch of the trail descends without hesitation to Santiago Oaks Regional Park). The way ahead is fraught with a confusing maze of powerline access roads and spurs; just make sure you fol-

Wind caves, overlooking Weir Canyon

low the markers for the regional trail, which are placed at all critical junctions.

At 0.8 mile (from the start) you pass near a high point long ago dubbed Robbers Peak. The name commemorates the notorious outlaws Joaquin Murietta, Three Finger Jack, and others of the late 1800s. Sweeping down out of the hills, these bandits terrorized the farmers below and preyed upon passengers traveling the Butterfield Stage. From Robbers Peak they could easily spot and evade sheriff's posses by slipping into the rugged ravines and canyons (including Weir Canyon) leading back toward the Santa Ana Mountains. From this height, you get a panoramic view of the lowlands to the south and west—a composite of soon-to-disappear pastoral landscapes and spreading suburban sprawl. On clear days, the panorama includes the blue arc of the Pacific Ocean and Santa Catalina Island.

Ahead on the trail lies a seemingly endless succession of twists and turns and ups and downs of various gradients. A rich assemblage of sage-scrub vegetation, dotted here and there with coast live oaks, smothers the slopes hereabouts. Strangely weathered sedimentary strata crop out in many places along the trail, lending an otherworldly feel to the journey—especially when seen in early-morning mist. Throughout the Peralta Hills, outcrops such as these provide nesting sites for swifts, hawks and other birds.

At 2.2 miles, signs indicate two choices; the way ahead is a 3.6-mile loop, so you'll return to this point later. To go counterclockwise around the loop make a sharp right, proceed 0.1 mile to a fenceline, and make a left on a trail going up a hill. Immediately to the left you'll spot a pair of closely spaced wind caves carved into a massive outcrop like the vacant eye sockets of a human skull. Shallow Weir Canyon lies below, perfectly quiet for now, but probably not for long. Two major roads, Weir Canyon Road and the Eastern Transportation Corridor toll road, will pass and east and south of here by the year 2000.

After a very crooked passage going northeast some 2 miles, in and out of ravines, the trail curves left and starts trending southwest, generally following a ridgeline. In places, fingers of suburbia reach upward toward the trail from the north, but there's no access to the streets below. When you return to the aforementioned junction—the start of the loop—you retrace your steps back to Serrano Avenue.

Trip 4: Irvine Regional Park

Distance	2 miles
Hiking Time	1 hour
Optional Map	USGS 7.5-min *Orange, Black Star Canyon*
Best Times	All year
Agency	IRP
Difficulty	★

For more than a century, Irvine Park has drawn Orange Countians up into the foothills of the Santa Ana Mountains. Once a meeting place for the early settlers—then known as the Picnic Grounds—it became Orange County Park in 1897 when early rancher James Irvine donated 160 acres of prime oak and sycamore groves fronting Santiago Creek. Today's park, now called Irvine Regional Park, has grown to 477 acres and hosts thousands of visitors on busy weekends.

Aside from picnic and playground areas, a boating lagoon, a small zoo, wildlife and historical exhibits, and various concessions (such as horse stables), it is possible to find some off-the-beaten-path hiking here. Several miles of paved and unpaved trails suitable for bicycling, hiking, and/or horse riding follow Santiago Creek and wind around the perimeter of the park.

If you don't want to share the park with hundreds of others, simply come on a weekday or on a winter weekend. It's surprising how colorful the park can be in the rainy "off season," and how little visited to boot. For a nice, short introduction on foot, try this:

Start at the Nature Trail parking area (bear right after passing the entrance station to reach it). Head up the paved path a short Distance to the first diversion—the William Harding Nature Area. Here a 0.3-mile self-guiding trail cut into a shady, north-facing hillside introduces you to some of the common chaparral and oak-woodland shrubs and trees.

On the paved path again, continue east along the perimeter of the park until you reach a split. Bear left and head across Santiago Creek on a concrete crossing. Despite its nearly 100 square miles of drainage, the creek's broad, open bed is almost always dry partly because much of the upstream surface flow has already seeped into porous soils, and partly because Santiago Reservoir impounds water upstream. There's still enough water underground, however, to keep the oaks, sycamores and other trees in the park looking healthy. The biggest oaks in the park are as old as 800 years.

On the far side of the creek, before you reach a small outcrop of sandstone, a dirt road (marked for horses) veers right to climb a dry bluff. Take this and continue about 0.4 mile to the "lookout," a small shade ramada overlooking the park, a good place for a restful pause or a bite to eat.

Complete the circuit by heading down the log stairway toward the walk-in picnic area below, and then crossing the creekbed via a paved path. If time allows, you can wander at length among the park's central attractions, all of which are clustered around the lagoon.

Trip 5: Peters Canyon Regional Park

Distance	3.8 miles (including Peters Canyon Creek Trail)
Total Elevation Gain/Loss	400'/400'
Hiking Time	2 hours
Optional Map	USGS 7.5-min *Orange*
Best Times	All year
Agency	SORP
Difficulty	★★

Deeded to Orange County by the Irvine Company in 1992, Peters Canyon Regional Park has, like other newly declared open-space areas, gained almost instant popularity among lovers of the outdoors. The park features the 55-acre Upper Peters Canyon Reservoir, several natural habitats (freshwater marsh, riparian woodland, grassland, and coastal sage-scrub), and about 6 miles of trails. The shallow reservoir is not open to fishing, but birding is fine here. Mats of marsh vegetation and water-loving trees (willows, cottonwoods, and sycamores) hug most of the shoreline, attracting egrets, grebes, herons, and other birds. The park is open from 7 A.M. to sunset daily.

From the park's northern (main) entrance and parking lot, off Canyon View Avenue in the city of Orange, you can start hiking by going west on the Lake View Trail. The shortest circumnavigation of the lake measures less than 2 miles, while side trips to the south, below the reservoir dam, can easily add another 2 miles. The highlight of the longer hike suggested here is the 0.8-mile Peters Canyon Creek Trail, which diverges from the main trail down along Peters Canyon (Lower Canyon Trail) about 300 yards south of the dam. This primitive trail, for hikers only, resembles a scaled-up rabbit run through the brush. You duck under the limbs of willow, black cottonwood, and sycamore, inhale the humid odors of riparian vegetation and the pungent scent of eucalyptus, and sometimes (depending on the

Peters Canyon Reservoir

season) splash through shallow water or squish through mud in the canyon bottom. Footbridges are provided at some of the creek crossings.

At the end of the Peters Canyon Creek Trail, you come up out of the shady canyon bottom to join the Lower Canyon Trail. By turning left there, you travel expeditiously north, up along the reservoir's east side and around the rest of the lake, toward your starting point. As you approach the north end of the lake, don't miss the narrow short-cut trail—through a dense growth of willows—on the left.

Area F-3: Whiting Ranch Wilderness Park

In 1991, Orange County opened to the public its newest large open-space preserve—Whiting Ranch Wilderness Park—in the foothills of the Santa Ana Mountains. Currently encompassing some 1500 acres along the rim of the communities of Lake Forest and El Toro, the park is likely to grow dramatically in the next decade or two when thousands of acres of Irvine Company land to the north pass into public ownership in exchange for development rights elsewhere in the county.

Whiting Ranch's rounded hills look a bit dry and nondescript when viewed from the suburbs below, but up close they reveal some pleasant surprises. One surprise is found in the upper reaches of a narrow ravine formerly inaccessible to the public: there stand some strangely weathered outcrops of red-tinted sandstone, rising sheer 100 feet or more. Some people optimistically refer to this natural amphitheater as Orange County's "Little Grand Canyon." The park is also noteworthy for its dense riparian and oak woodland vegetation which smothers the bottoms of the park's larger ravines.

To reach the park's main entrance from Interstate 5 in southern Orange County, take Lake Forest Drive east and north for 5 miles to Portola Parkway, turn left, and follow Portola northwest for another ½ mile. Look for a trailhead parking area on the right, just beyond a shopping center. The lot is open from 7 A.M. to sunset. Another parking lot serving the park is located on Glenn Ranch Road. A brochure and trail map for the park is available at either trailhead, and maps or directional signs posted at critical trail junctions help make navigation on the trail system easy.

Trip 1: Borrego Canyon to Red Rock

Distance	4.0 miles
Total Elevation Gain/Loss	500'/500'
Hiking Time	2 hours (round trip)
Optional Maps	USGS 7.5-min *El Toro*
Best Times	October through June
Agency	WRWP
Difficulty	★★

From the main parking lot on Portola Parkway, the Borrego Trail leads straightway to Red Rock canyon, where sandstone cliffs banded with layers of ancient sand and mud rise into the air. The best illumination of the cliffs usually occurs late in the day, when the sun's warm glow brings out the ruddy tint of oxidized iron on the surface of the rock.

Like most trails in the Whiting Ranch Wilderness Park, the Borrego Trail is open to mountain biking and horse riding, as well as hiking. You immediately plunge into densely shaded Borrego Canyon, alongside a stream that happily trickles through during winter and spring. For a while, suburbia rims the canyon on both sides, but soon enough it disappears without a trace. The trek up the canyon feels Tolkienesque as you pass under a crooked-limb canopy of live oaks and sycamores, and sniff the damp odor of the streamside

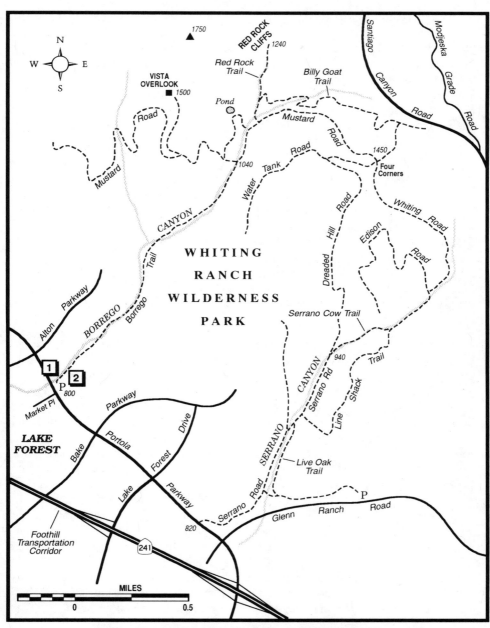

Area F-3: Whiting Ranch Wilderness Park

willows. Often in the late fall and winter, frigid air sinks into these shady recesses overnight, and by early morning frost mantles everything below eye-level.

After no more than about 40 minutes of walking and 1.3 miles, you come to Mustard Road, a fire road that ascends both east and west to ridgetops offering long views of the ocean on clear days. Turn right on Mustard Road, pass a picnic site, and take the second trail to the left (the Red Rock Trail—for hikers only), into an up-

per tributary of Borrego Canyon.

Out in the sunshine now, you meander up the bottom of a sunny ravine that becomes increasingly narrow and steep. Presently, you reach the base of the eroded sandstone cliffs, formed of sediment deposited on a shallow sea bottom about 20 million years ago. This type of rock, which contains the fossilized remains of shellfish and marine mammals, underlies much of Orange County. Rarely is it as well exposed as here.

Trip 2: Whiting Ranch Loop

Distance	5.5 miles
Total Elevation Gain/Loss	800'/800'
Hiking Time	3 hours
Optional Map	USGS 7.5-min *El Toro*
Best Times	October through May
Agency	WRWP
Difficulty	★★★

For a more comprehensive survey of Whiting Ranch park, try this circle hike through the park's two largest canyons. You'll travel up Borrego Canyon to a watershed divide, then descend through Serrano Canyon. The basic loop measures 5.5 miles (including a mile on the sidewalk along Portola Parkway at the end), though numerous side trips and extensions are possible if you want to lengthen your hike.

Start by heading up Borrego Canyon from Portola Parkway. At 1.3 miles you meet Mustard Road. Turn right. (To the left, Mustard Road would take you up along grassy slopes to the west, smothered in yellow mustard in the spring). Continue on Mustard Road, going north and later east, up the main tributary of Borrego Can-

yon to Four Corners (2.2 miles), where four road segments join at a saddle. (A more roundabout way of reaching Four Corners could involve the Billy Goat Trail, a rough path to the north with constant and often severe ups and downs, and not much shade).

At Four Corners, go across to Whiting Road and start descending—gradually at first along a ridge, then more steeply off the ridge and into an oak-lined valley (upper Serrano Canyon). From now on, simply maintain your descent at all junctions, following the Serrano Cow Trail through a sublime tunnel of live oaks and finally the Serrano Road out to Portola Parkway. From there follow the sidewalk a mile back to your starting point.

Area F-4: O'Neill Regional Park/ Mission Viejo

Encompassing more than 3000 acres of riparian bottomlands, oak woodlands, grassy meadows, and scrub-covered hills, O'Neill Regional Park is one of the oldest parks in Orange County. Starting with 278 acres donated in 1948 by the descendants of the O'Neill family (owners of what was once a vast ranching empire stretching across southern Orange County), the park grew steadily to accommodate the needs of the expanding county population. A nice complement of recreational facilities was developed: picnic tables, a playground, a ball field, a small arboretum, and camping areas for equestrians and motorists. Later additions to the park west of Live Oak Canyon Road made possible the development of an extensive trail system for hikers, horseback riders, and mountain bikers.

The most recent acquisition, the 935-acre Arroyo Trabuco Wilderness, lay off-limits for more than a decade before it opened for public use in 1995. Its long, curvilinear form, stretching almost 6 miles through the rapidly expanding suburban landscape of Mission Viejo, serves as an important wildlife corridor between the Santa Ana Mountains and the still-undeveloped parts of coastal Orange County. This and other long, narrow strips of open space throughout this growing part of the county are being preserved in perpetuity as greenbelts.

South of O'Neill Park, another patch of open space, laden with trails, welcomes you. This 475-acre parcel, Thomas F. Riley Wilderness Park (formerly Wagon Wheel Canyon Regional Park), was deeded to the county in 1983 by the developers of the adjacent community of Coto de Caza. Not until easy access was assured (by way of the new, east extension of Oso Parkway) was the park opened for public use in December 1994. The Riley Park trails are described in Trip 4 in the following section.

Once remote from civilization, O'Neill Park now lies close to a network of major roads threading through Mission Viejo. To reach the park's entrance, head south on Live Oak Canyon Road from where it joins with El Toro Road and Santiago Canyon Road, and continue for 3 miles. Another route is by way of Santa Margarita Parkway and Plano Trabuco Road. Upon reaching the park's entrance and office, pay the day-use fee and park in any of the nearby day-use or picnic areas. Day users are welcome from 7 A.M. to sunset. For those interested in overnight camping, O'Neill Park offers 93 campsites on a first-come, first-served basis.

Riley Wilderness Park is open for day use only (7 A.M. to sunset). The park can be expeditiously reached from Interstate 5 by driving 6 miles east on Oso Parkway. A dirt driveway, on the right, leads to a parking area (fee charged) where several trails originate.

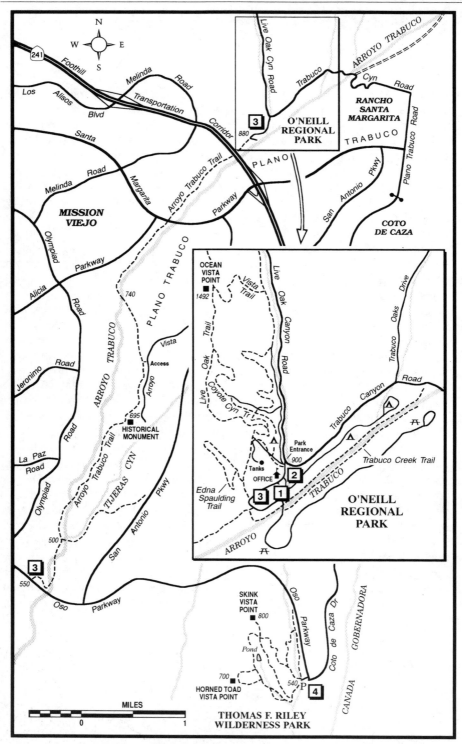

Area F-4: O'Neill Regional Park/Mission Viejo

Trip 1: Trabuco Creek Trail

	Distance	1.5 miles
	Hiking Time	1 hour (round trip)
	Optional Map	USGS 7.5-min *Santiago Peak*
	Best Times	All year
	Agency	ONRP
	Difficulty	★

This short, flat, self-guiding nature trail, with stations keyed to a leaflet available at the O'Neill Regional Park office, runs through a narrow strip of oak woodland on the south side of Arroyo Trabuco ("Trabuco Creek"), the major drainage through the park. After parking near the office or at any adjacent day-use (not camping) area, follow the road heading toward the Featherly and Mesa day-use areas. It fords the cobbled arroyo bed, and the trail begins on the far bank, on the left.

Whereas the north bank of Arroyo Trabuco is nothing but a gravel berm built up to control flood waters, the south bank has been left under nature's control. You'll be walking between the open bed of the creek and the base of a mesalike formation to the south called Plano Trabuco ("Trabuco Flat" or "Trabuco Plain"), a terrace made up of alluvial deposits cast off of the Santa Ana Mountains. Over recent geologic time, the abrasive floodwaters of Arroyo Trabuco have cut about 100 feet deep into Plano Trabuco's soft sediments, creating a clifflike slope. These same floodwaters, however, have deposited enough fertile sediment on the bank to support the lush growth of trees and shrubs. You tend to lose sight of civilization on the trail, though just above, spreading across the 5-mile-long Plano Trabuco, stand the red-tile-roofed community of

Rancho Santa Margarita and other massive housing developments of the present and near future.

Plano Trabuco acquired its name in 1769, when a soldier traveling with the Portola expedition lost a blunderbuss (trabuco) there. A string of contemporary place names are descended from the original: Arroyo Trabuco, Trabuco Canyon (the community), Trabuco Canyon (the head of Arroyo Trabuco in the Santa Ana Moun-

On the Trabuco Creek Trail

tains), and the Trabuco Ranger District (the part of Cleveland National Forest that en-

compasses the Santa Ana Mountains).

Trip 2: Ocean Vista Point

Distance	3.0 miles
Total Elevation Gain/Loss	650'/650'
Hiking Time	1½ hours
Optional Map	USGS 7.5-min *Santiago Peak*
Best Times	All year
Agency	ONRP
Difficulty	★★

An inspiring vista of sea on one side, and chaparral- and sage-covered mountains on the other, awaits you at the midpoint of this hike. Don't forget binoculars and perhaps a county map to familiarize yourself with Orange County's urban and natural geography.

From O'Neill Park's entrance, walk north on the paved service road that runs parallel to Live Oak Canyon Road. Almost

immediately, bear left on another paved road leading to some hilltop water tanks. After about 0.3 mile, leave the pavement and veer right onto a dirt road—the Live Oak Trail. After swinging around two hairpin turns, go left at the next fork, staying on Live Oak Trail. This road takes you up to and then along the top of a viewful ridgeline. Your destination, a 1492-foot bump on the ridge ahead called the Ocean

Arroyo Trabuco and Plano Trabuco (left) from Santiago Peak. O'Neill Park at lower center

Vista Point, may be identified from afar by a spiky cellular-telephone antenna structure near its top.

Breezy days from late fall to early spring are best for the view. Often visible above the usual smog layer are San Clemente and Santa Catalina islands, the Palos Verdes peninsula, and the Santa Monica Mountains. To the east, the Santa Ana Mountains rise impressively, so much more so because you look *down* on their lower flanks, as well as up to their summits.

To make this a loop trip, follow the Vista Trail east (and steadily downhill) toward Live Oak Canyon. Bear right at the bottom and follow an old, mostly paved service road paralleling Live Oak Canyon Road. Continue south (very gradually downhill) until you reach your starting point.

Trip 3: Arroyo Trabuco

Distance	5.8 miles
Total Elevation Gain/Loss	170'/500'
Hiking Time	3 hours
Optional Maps	USGS 7.5-min *Santiago Peak, Canada Gobernadora, San Juan Capistrano*
Best Times	October through June
Agency	ONRP
Difficulty	★★★

The somewhat long but easy-going trek down the Arroyo Trabuco is most adventurous just after winter rainy periods, when turbid water dances over a wide, gravelly bed, and there's no way to avoid a good foot-soaking at each of four fords you encounter along the trail. Generally, the O'Neill Park rangers prohibit the use of the Arroyo Trabuco Wilderness section during rainstorms, and may limit its use just afterward—so be sure to check first.

By early April, waist-high green grass pokes upward from the soft ground and the emerging leaves on the sycamores flutter on the marine air that persistently pushes its way inland. Blooming mustard and poppies appear as April grades into May—just as the grass bleaches to yellow or brown. By summer the arroyo creekbed is usually dry, and the midday heat can be oppressive. The scenery improves greatly in November and December as the sycamore leaves turn crispy and yellow and drift earthward on capricious puffs of Santa Ana wind.

This trip being (in its most simple form) a one-way hike, arrange to be dropped off at O'Neill Park and later picked up along Oso Parkway, just west of the long bridge over Arroyo Trabuco. Currently no parking is provided at the end of the trail, though a concrete apron allows westbound cars to pull off the parkway at that spot. A future trailhead is planned for somewhere near Oso Parkway; consult with O'Neill Park rangers to get the latest information.

Begin at the west end of the Oak Grove day-use area, west of the O'Neill Park office, where the well-marked trail down along the Arroyo Trabuco begins. You soon pass under a massive twin bridge (Foothill Transportation Corridor toll road) and later pass under another equally huge bridge (Santa Margarita Parkway). As an environmental mitigation for the construction of these bridges, county workers and volunteers have planted on the arroyo banks more than 2000 native trees and shrubs—live oak, sycamore, toyon, mulefat, and willow. Barring future floods, this upper stretch of the arroyo may look better than ever a decade or two hence.

Solitude in Arroyo Trabuco Wilderness

At 1.9 miles, well past the second bridge, the trail swings left across the creek and ascends moderately toward the lip of the gorge and toward new houses built upon Plano Trabuco. The trail sidles up to Arroyo Vista (a street with houses on the far side), where there is a signed access point for the trail. Plenty of curbside parking is here, if you want to plan a shorter trip up or down the arroyo. A mile ahead, the trail descends back into the gorge. On the left, before you begin the descent, notice a small structure accompanied by a historical plaque. This marks the campsite, designated San Francisco Solano, which was used by the Portola expedition on the night of July 24–25, 1769.

After the descent, the trail continues for another 2 miles down alongside the wide floodplain, always staying close to the streambed. This is the most agreeable part of the canyon, with gnarled sycamores and oaks alternating with grassy clearings. After three stream crossings, the Oso Parkway bridge looms high overhead. Underneath it you can pick up a powerline access road up the left (west) slope of the arroyo, and ascend to reach the shoulder of Oso Parkway.

Trip 4: Riley Wilderness Park

Distance	3.0 miles
Total Elevation Gain/Loss	350'/350'
Hiking Time	1½ hours
Optional Maps	USGS 7.5-min *Canada Gobernadora*
Best Times	All year
Agency	CWP
Difficulty	★★

Thomas F. Riley Wilderness Park, a wilderness in name only, spreads over 475 acres of rolling hills and oak-lined ravines, and includes about 5 miles of trails open to hikers, equestrians, and mountain bikers. Like much of Orange County's foothills, this area was until recently home to far more cattle than people. Hardly pristine in a biological sense, the park none-theless preserves a pocket of open space that will permanently resist the bulldozer blade. Currently, a vast stretch of land to the north and east is being reshaped by giant earth movers, and someday the Foot-hill Transportation Corridor toll road will slice along the ridge just west of the park.

The following moderately easy trek around the park's perimeter is rewarding. From the parking lot, head north on oak-shaded Wagon Wheel Canyon Trail, which runs parallel to Oso Parkway. After 0.4 mile, turn left, cross the shallow bottom of Wagon Wheel Canyon, and double back south on Pheasant Run Trail. After a gentle rise and a fall you arrive at the Mule Deer Trail, nearly back at the starting point. Make a sharp right and start climbing again. Early spring brings forth a good dis-play of wildflowers on the grassy hillsides ahead: shooting stars, lupine, wild hya-cinth, and monkey flower. Later in the spring, blooming mustard paints yellow patches across these slopes.

The crooked climb on the Mule Deer Trail leads toward a ridgetop trail junction. Skink Vista Point, offering a somewhat wider view of the park and its surround-ings, lies on the bald ridgeline a little higher and farther north of that junction. Jog left a little and turn right, starting a short and sharp descent into a shallow val-ley. Proceed south down the valley past a old stock pond, noting the sign for Horned Toad Vista Point on the right. The short and steep side trip up through aromatic sage-scrub vegetation is worth it; from the top of the trail you can gaze down on the most pristine and secluded parts of the park.

Returning to the previous trail, turn right and descend toward the oak- and sycamore-dotted floor of the valley. By staying right at all subsequent junctions you will return to the parking lot, ap-proaching it from the south.

Wagon Wheel Canyon

Area F-5: Caspers Wilderness Park

Caspers Wilderness Park is without a doubt the crown jewel of Orange County's regional park system. It is the largest park established to date in the county, the least altered by human activities, and the most remote from population centers. Its position adjacent to Cleveland National Forest on the east and north, and the Audubon Society's Starr Ranch Sanctuary on the north and west, integrates it into the only good-sized area within Orange County that could truthfully be called a wilderness. Caspers wouldn't qualify as a statutory wilderness (that is, roadless and primitive) area by federal standards, as does nearby San Mateo Canyon Wilderness, but the richness of its wildlife is testimony enough to its *de facto* primitive state.

Strangely enough, the area encompassing Caspers Park—the former Starr Ranch—narrowly escaped development as a commercial amusement park back in the early '70s. Fortunately, the owners of the property at the time went bankrupt. Instead, most of the north half of the property was deeded to the Audubon Society in 1973. The south half was purchased by Orange County in 1974 for use as a regional park, largely through the efforts of Board of Supervisors chairman Ronald W. Caspers. Subsequent purchases increased the total park area to its present 7600 acres.

True to the vision of those who foresaw Caspers Park as protecting one of Orange County's last natural areas and as being a great recreation resource as well, the park today is graced with a fine complement of facilities and improvements. The beautiful visitor center houses a small museum and an open-air loft offering spectacular views of the Santa Ana

Mountains. The camping and picnic facilities are second to none in Orange County; a separate area is included for equestrians. Radiating out to the outer reaches of the park are more than 30 miles of riding and hiking trails.

Tragically, Caspers Park was the scene of two separate mountain lion attacks on small children in 1986. Such incidents are considered rare; nonetheless, legal actions against the county by the parents of the injured children have resulted in the closure of the park's campgrounds and trails to kids under 18. This no-minors policy has remained in effect for a decade. Adults may use any trail within the park, but must obtain a wilderness permit for that privilege first.

Protection and enhancement of natural habitat are among the park's most important goals. To this end firebreaks have been constructed on some of the ridges in order to facilitate controlled burns. Periodic burning favors native plants over the non-native grasses and weedy plants introduced in the past, and helps to maintain the natural sage-scrub vegetation, which is well adapted to fire. Parts of these firebreaks have been incorporated into the trail system, which also includes dirt maintenance roads and footpaths. A firestorm in October 1993 (one of several simultaneous fires that burned throughout Southern California) swept the northeastern two-thirds of the park, but did not destroy any of the park's visitor facilities.

To reach Caspers Park, drive 7.6 miles east from Interstate 5 on Ortega Highway (Highway 74). Beyond the clearly marked entrance (pay a fee and fill out a permit here), drive up upon the knoll a short distance ahead to reach the visitor

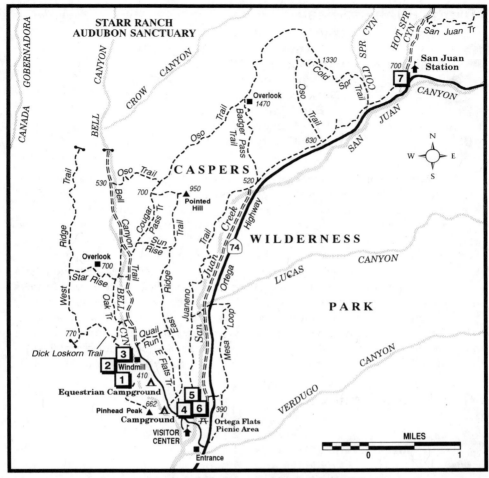

Area F-5: Caspers Wilderness Park

center. Besides visiting the museum and the loft, you can loop around the 0.1-mile-long Vista Ridge self-guiding trail south of the parking lot. There you'll be introduced to the common vegetation of the area as well as the geographic setting.

Several days could be spent exploring the rest of the trail system, which will take you through two basic kinds of environments: (1) the always impressive oak-and-sycamore woodlands along San Juan and Bell canyons (the two largest drainages in the park); and (2) the sage- and chaparral-covered hillsides offering, on clear days at least, magnificent views stretching from the ocean to the Santa Ana Mountains. You can start with one of the following.

Trip 1: Pinhead Peak

Distance	1.5 miles
Total Elevation Gain/Loss	400'/400'
Hiking Time	1 hour (round trip)
Optional Map	USGS 7.5-min *Canada Gobernadora*
Best Times	All year
Agency	CWP
Difficulty	★

The view from the visitor center is impressive, but from Pinhead Peak it's even better. Here you can look down on the three-way confluence of dry creekbeds San Juan, Bell, and Verdugo and spot the toylike visitor center perched atop the knoll between the first two.

You may pick up the trail, an ill-defined footpath at first, at either the equestrian camping area or the old windmill site a little farther north. Travel south across a meadow into a grassy cove, then follow a better-defined trail up the scrub-covered ridge on the left. After a short but vigorous climb, you'll reach a high point on the ridge next to a wire fence defining the park boundary. This is the 662-foot peak called "Pinhead." The trail continues 200 yards to a slightly lower bump on the ridge offering a more panoramic view. From both peaks almost the entire extent of Caspers Park can be seen. Successively higher ridges lead the eye northward and eastward toward the two summits of Old Saddleback and other notable promontories in the southern Santa Ana Mountains.

Trip 2: Oak Trail Loop

Distance	2.1 miles
Total Elevation Gain/Loss	150'/150'
Hiking Time	1 hour
Optional Map	USGS 7.5-min *Canada Gobernadora*
Best Times	All year
Agency	CWP
Difficulty	★

Magnificent coast live oak trees, the biggest in the park, line this trail along the west side of Bell Canyon. The Spanish called this tree *la encina*, a word whose derivatives are echoed in the communities of Encino near Los Angeles and Encinitas ("little oaks") near San Diego.

Start at the old windmill (a mile north by paved road from the visitor center), following the path signed NATURE TRAIL. Cross the gravelly bed of Bell Canyon and stay on the far side for the next 1.0 mile.

As if stricken with some kind of arboreal arthritis, the limbs and branches of the oaks are fantastically contorted. Actually there's an underlying order to the seemingly random pattern. By intricately branching, the tree can support more leaves with less wood. Many of the oaks show fire scars dating back to the Stewart fire of 1958, which originated in Riverside County. Pushed along by Santa Ana winds, the fire swept across all of what is now Caspers Park, charring a total of 66,000 acres. This

On the Oak Trail

area was not quite reached by the 1993 fire, which also swept southwest on a Santa Ana, but stalled about a mile from here.

In late fall the tall sycamores along the Oak Trail can be even more attractive than the oaks. Crunch through the crispy leaf litter beneath their spreading crowns and watch the golden sunbeams dance amid thousands of fluttering leaves overhead. In winter the trunks and branches are ghostly white. By early spring, new leaves are emerging, and sunlight passing though them bathes the ground shadows in a jungle-green luminance.

When you reach Star Rise (the fire road coming down from Bell Canyon's west ridge) turn right. After 100 feet, bear right again on a foot trail leading over to the Bell Canyon Trail, a dirt road. You can follow this back about a mile to the starting point.

Trip 3: West Ridge-Bell Canyon Loop

	Distance	3.3 miles
	Total Elevation Gain/Loss	400'/400'
	Hiking Time	1½ hours
	Optional Map	USGS 7.5-min *Canada Gobernadora*
	Best Times	October through June
	Agency	CWP
	Difficulty	★★

This hike features a rather dizzying passage across the top of some curious white sandstone formations, rather like the breaks along the upper Missouri River or the barren cliffs of the South Dakota badlands. You'll loop up and over the main ridge defining the west edge of the park, enjoying views of adjacent areas of the county not ordinarily seen from any road.

Begin hiking at the old windmill (a mile north by paved road from the visitor center) on a path signed NATURE TRAIL. Follow it across the wide bed of Bell Canyon and into the dense oak woodland on the far side. After 0.3 mile you'll spot a park bench beneath a gorgeous, spreading oak tree. A little farther on, veer left on the Dick Loskorn Trail. This path meanders up a shallow draw and soon climbs to a sandstone ridgeline that at one point narrows to near-knife-edge width. At one point you step within a foot of a modest but unnerving abyss. The sandstone is part of a marine sedimentary formation, called the Santiago Formation (roughly 45 million years old), which crops out along the coastal strip from here down to mid-San Diego County.

After climbing about 350 feet, you come to a dirt road—the West Ridge Trail. Turn north, skirting the fence line of Rancho Mission Viejo, a vast landholding that encompasses much of southern Orange County and formerly included (before World War II) all of Camp Pendleton as well. To the left and right there are good views of both Bell Canyon and Canada Gobernadora ("Canyon of the Governor's Wife"—though a less literal meaning refers to the invasive chamise, or greasewood, that used to fill the canyon). Canada Gobernadora is now largely given over to agriculture and to the exclusive Coto de Caza housing development. The confluence of Canada Gobernadora and San Juan Canyon is one of several supposed sites for Mission Vieja, the original San Juan Capistrano Mission, founded in 1776.

After 0.7 mile on the West Ridge Trail, turn right on Star Rise—the road descending toward Bell Canyon. On the left is a flat terrace, the site of a disused trail campground, with a commanding view of almost the entire park. From a park bench perched on the edge of the terrace you can look down on the line of oaks and sycamores in the canyon below.

From the bottom of the grade on Star Rise, you can return to the starting point using either of the two parallel trails going downhill through Bell Canyon—the Oak and Bell Canyon trails.

Trip 4: East Ridge-Bell Canyon Loop

Distance	6.7 miles
Total Elevation Gain/Loss	900'/900'
Hiking Time	3 hours
Optional Map	USGS 7.5-min *Canada Gobernadora*
Best Times	October through May
Agency	CWP
Difficulty	★★

On this hike you'll pass through two very different kinds of natural habitat: first, a scruffy mix of drought-resistant coastal sage-scrub and chaparral plants on the sunny hillsides and ridges; second, the moisture-loving oak-and-sycamore woodlands along Bell Canyon.

From just north of the entrance to the San Juan Meadow picnic area, follow the East Flats Trail uphill for 0.2 mile. Bear right at an intersection and climb on the East Ridge Trail (a wide firebreak), which soon gains a well-defined ridgeline and then sticks to it for the next 2 miles or so. Dead ahead lies the summit of Santiago Peak, some 10 miles north and almost a mile higher.

Aside from the usual California sagebrush, white sage, black sage, and laurel sumac of the sage-scrub community, several common chaparral-community plants make their appearance as you climb: chamise, toyon, yucca, deerweed, manzanita, and elderberry. You'll also pass some dense thickets of prickly pear cactus, native to these hills but probably more widespread today because of past overgrazing.

At 2.7 miles from the start the firebreak comes up just short of a knoll to the east—Pointed Hill. Walk over to it and you'll be treated to a grand view up San Juan Canyon toward the higher Santa Anas.

Next, go back to East Ridge and descend the grassy slope to the west, using a firebreak. At the bottom, turn right on the Cougar Pass Trail and continue 0.2 mile through a cluster of oaks to the intersection of the Oso Trail, where you turn left toward Bell Canyon. After a little climbing you level off and begin crossing a grassy terrace before dropping again. This flat area is a remnant of one of three or four ancient "river" terraces exposed on the wall of Bell Canyon. Each terrace represents a stage when Bell Creek became stabilized and used most of its energy to widen its bed rather than cut a deeper channel. Between these quiescent stages, tectonic uplift or other factors, such as a change to a wetter climate, rejuvenated the creek, which then rapidly cut itself to a lower level. Today the creek is engaged in a period of widening, as evidenced by the canyon's broad, flat floor.

Upon reaching the canyon floor, turn left on the Bell Canyon Trail and follow it all the way back to the pavement and your starting point. In the winter, surface water tumbles through the upper part of the canyon but seldom reaches its mouth. The headwaters lie in a rugged and almost inaccessible gorge below Los Pinos Peak in Cleveland National Forest (see Area M-2, Trip 7).

On the drier benches alongside the canyon bottom (themselves recent river-terrace features) you'll find some coast cholla cactus along with the more familiar prickly pear; various sage-scrub and chaparral plants; and naturalized non-natives typical of heavily grazed or disturbed areas, such as wild oats and rye grass, filaree, mustard, artichoke thistle, milk thistle, and tree tobacco. Here, in the transition zone between the shady woodland along the creek and the warm, dry slopes, your chances of spotting wildlife and birds are greatest. Look for deer, coyotes, bobcats, mountain lions, and a host of smaller creatures. When the ground is wet, tracks easily give away their presence.

The name "Bell," incidentally, commemorates an eight-ton granitic boulder, scored with mazelike petroglyphs, that once lay precariously balanced on some smaller rocks, upstream in what is now the Audubon Sanctuary. When struck with great force, the boulder resonated like a bell, audible a mile away. Removed from the canyon in 1936, Bell Rock was taken to the courtyard of the Bowers Museum in Santa Ana, where it rests today.

Pointed Hill in Caspers Park

Trip 5: Oso Trail-Juaneno Trail Loop

	Distance	8.8 miles
	Total Elevation Gain/Loss	2200'/2200'
	Hiking Time	5 hours
	Optional Map	USGS 7.5-min *Canada Gobernadora*
	Best Times	November through April
	Agency	CWP
	Difficulty	★★★

Pick a clear, cool day, and set aside the better part of it for this hike to one of the highest ridges in the park. You'll have a wonderful view of the higher Santa Anas, the Los Angeles Basin, the San Joaquin Hills, and the ocean. You'll return along San Juan Creek, meandering in and out of the shade of oaks and sycamores.

Park at the San Juan Meadow picnic area, and begin by walking north up the paved road into Bell Canyon. Past the end of the pavement, continue north on the Bell Canyon Trail (dirt road) for one mile, then bear right on the Cougar Pass Trail. Continue northeast up and over a river-terrace remnant, briefly through a cluster of oaks, then (on the Oso Trail) straight up the spine of a ridge blanketed with prickly pear cacti. After blooming yellow, orange, or red in the spring and early summer, these cacti grow bulblike fruits, loaded with black seeds, along the edges of their paddle-shaped leaves. The fruits themselves, best displayed in October and November, exhibit a variety of bizarre colors best described as shades of purple, magenta, and red.

Up ahead on the brow of the ridge, a shade ramada with picnic table awaits the footsore. Here you can savor the beforementioned panoramic view. The Oso Trail continues ahead on the ridgeline, skirting the property line of Audubon's Starr Ranch Sanctuary.

From the overlook, our way now descends south along a crooked firebreak—the Badger Pass Trail—toward San Juan Creek. During one hike along this trail, just after a heavy rain, my companions and I had the comical experience of slopping down this slope with about five pounds of adobe-like soil clinging to each of our shoes. At the bottom of the firebreak, next to the Ortega Highway bridge over San Juan Creek, pick up the Juaneno Trail. Follow its narrow course downstream along the west side of the creek's usually dry flood plain.

On the Juaneno Trail

Over the next 3 miles the trail follows a scenic, not-so-direct route—sometimes along cobbled banks dotted with riparian vegetation, otherwise along upper terraces delightfully shaded by oak trees. Bluffs consisting of buff-colored marine sedimentary rock soar dramatically on your right.

At one point you circle a covelike indentation in the cliff wall, reminiscent of the stone amphitheaters in Zion National Park.

After a final detour up and over a wooded slope overlooking the flood plain, the trail emerges at the east end of San Juan Meadow picnic area, your starting point.

Trip 6: Mesa Loop

Distance	3.2 miles
Total Elevation Gain/Loss	200'/200'
Hiking Time	1½ hours
Optional Map	USGS 7.5-min *Canada Gobernadora*
Best Times	All year
Agency	CWP
Difficulty	★

Although you're never far from the highway on this trip, the sight and sounds of traffic are usually muted by vegetation and the peculiar topography. East of the highway, the stairstep profiles of the hillsides show the many levels of San Juan Creek's past courses. This route takes you along the best-preserved of these river-terrace formations (explained in Trip 4 above).

Begin at the Ortega Flats picnic area. Pick up the maintenance road to the north which angles toward Ortega Highway. After 0.2 mile you'll see a large culvert on the right. Pass under the highway through

this and find the dirt road on the far side. The road follows a pleasant, oak-dotted drainage for a short while, then swings left and climbs out of the drainage.

After a brief climb, you emerge atop the lowest and best-defined of the four terrace levels in this stretch of San Juan Canyon. Wildflowers thrive in silty soil by the trailside during spring and early summer. Beyond the lip of the terrace, the buff-colored cliffs along San Juan Creek form a picturesque backdrop.

Up ahead the terrace is cut by two small ravines, and then by a much bigger

Grasslands and sage scrub on the Oso Trail

break—Lucas Canyon. Nearing Lucas Canyon you come to a locked gate; a private inholding in the center of the park lies ahead. At the gate veer left onto a faint footpath leading west down to the highway. Pass under the highway again through a second culvert and work your way over to the far side of the open bed of San Juan Creek. Pick up the Juaneno Trail there and follow it through the oak groves back toward your starting point. When you reach a pumphouse along the trail, bear right toward the first culvert and return to the Ortega Flats picnic area.

Trip 7: Cold Spring Canyon Loop

Distance	4.2 miles
Total Elevation Gain/Loss	900'/900'
Hiking Time	2½ hours
Optional Map	USGS 7.5-min *Canada Gobernadora*
Best Times	October through June
Agency	CWP
Difficulty	★★

Filled with tall, slender alder trees and spreading oaks, Cold Spring Canyon used to be one of the most beautiful spots in Caspers Park. Today, signs of 1993's devastating wildfire are still very much in evidence, but much biological recovery has taken place, aided by two unusually wet winters following the fire.

On a north-facing slope just above Cold Spring Canyon, you'll get a wide-open view of rugged, brush-covered hillsides uncut by roads or trails or any other perceptible form of human alteration as far as the eye can see. Such refreshing vistas are rare things to be treasured in today's Orange County.

Unlike the other hikes in Caspers Park, this one begins at the site of San Juan Hot Springs, a privately owned resort that was totally incinerated during the October 1993 wildfire. Obtain your wilderness permit (available only at the park entrance) first, then drive 5 miles north on Ortega Highway to Hot Springs Canyon Road, on the left. Park at or near the fire station here and head west around the fenced hot springs site on whatever path you can find. After 0.3 mile you come to Cold Spring Canyon, a deep ravine with a stream flowing through during the wet half of the year.

Pick up the path known as the Cold Springs Trail and follow it up the canyon for 0.3 mile. The trail gains a toehold on the slope to the left and soon veers west up along the south wall of a ravine. In a decade or two, dense chaparral will blanket this slope and perhaps a profusion of ferns will too. Before the fire, as many as five varieties of fern could be found growing on a single square-yard plot. The view keeps expanding as you climb, and soon encompasses the pristine upper reaches of Cold Spring Canyon.

After 500 vertical feet of ascent, you meet the Oso Trail (a fire road). To make this hike a loop trip, stay left and continue west on the Oso Trail, which descends into and then along the bottom of a sunny canyon full of sage-scrub vegetation. Here there are hardy laurel sumacs, which waste no time is resprouting after fire—often before the next rainy season starts.

At the bottom of the Oso Trail turn left, parallel to Ortega Highway, and follow a wide firebreak east. The firebreak soon turns abruptly up a ridge to the north. After climbing about 100 feet, look for a narrow foot trail to the right. This trail contours over to the mouth of Cold Spring Canyon, where you pick up the path leading back to your starting point.

Area F-6: Santa Rosa Plateau Ecological Reserve

The Santa Rosa Plateau, on a southeastern spur of the Santa Ana Mountains, rises over the rapidly expanding suburban communities of southwest Riverside County like a Shangri-La in the sky. In the early '80s hardly anyone knew of its existence or its ecological significance. Starting with a nucleus of 3100 acres purchased by The Nature Conservancy from a housing-development company in 1983, the current ecological reserve on the plateau now includes more than 8000 acres—some 13 square miles. Several public agencies have joined The Nature Conservancy in managing today's reserve, including (strangely enough) the Metropolitan Water District of Southern California. Though the area lies far from any significant source of water, the MWD's purchase and management of lands added to the preserve are offsetting natural habitat losses due to MWD's construction of the giant Domenigoni Reservoir 20 miles away.

A circle, 100 miles in radius, centered on the reserve, encompasses a megalopolis of some 20 million people. File this fact away in your mind, and then try to fathom its truth while walking amid the green and golden hills of this exquisitely beautiful place. Here is a classic California landscape of wind-rippled grasses, swaying poppies, statuesque oak trees, trickling streams, vernal pools, and a dazzling assortment of native plants (469 at last count) and animals. You will be struck by the reserve's timelessness and insularity, and you will quickly realize how important it was to save it.

Most of the newly purchased sections of the reserve are closed to visitors, though the older (west half) of the reserve is laced with newer trails as well as old ranch roads open to hiking. Horseback riding and

Englemann oak, Santa Rosa Plateau

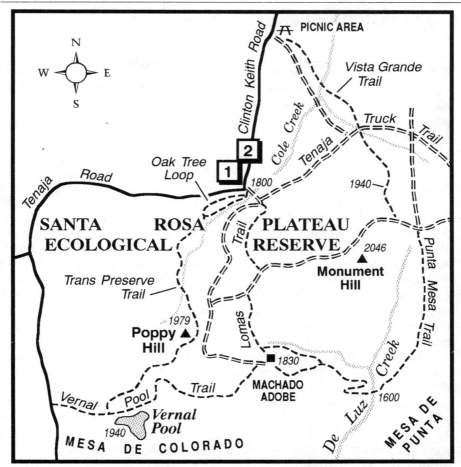

Area F-6: Santa Rosa Plateau

mountain biking are restricted, though tours featuring these modes of travel are occasionally offered. A multi-use trail running along the perimeter of the reserve and into suburban Murrieta in the valley below is being planned. In addition, the 1996 purchase of an adjacent ranch to the west (Sylvan Meadows) has opened up the possibility of constructing user facilities—such as an interpretive center, picnic areas, and mountain bike trails—on lands less sensitive than those in the main reserve.

From most parts of Orange County, the reserve can be reached in just over an hour by taking Highway 91 east to Interstate 15 in Corona, and I-15 southeast to the Clinton Keith Road exit in Murrieta. Turn right and head south on Clinton Keith Road 5 miles to the new reserve main entrance, picnic area, and visitor center. Note that this new entrance for hikes 1 and 2 replaces the one indicated on the map above; this new entrance is now at the picnic area on Clinton Keith Road. Hikers can use the northern leg of the Vista Grande Trail to reach hikes 1 and 2. There is now a charge to visit the preserve; $2 for adults and $1 for children.

Every Southern Californian should have at least one chance to see the Santa Rosa Plateau reserve at its stunning best—during March and April, following a wet winter. Mark your calendar now!

Trip 1: Oak Tree Loop

Distance	0.7 mile
Hiking Time	½ hour
Optional Map	USGS 7.5-min *Wildomar*
Best Times	All year
Agency	SRPER
Difficulty	★

The self-guiding Oak Tree Trail (a loop trail with leaflets available at the start) takes you through what is billed as the only protected, self-reproducing stand of Engelmann oaks remaining on Earth. The Engelmann oak (or mesa oak), native to the coastal foothills of Southern California and far-northern Baja California, is rapidly being displaced by urbanization and other forms of habitat degradation. These trees are easily distinguishable from their botanical cousins and frequent neighbors—coast live oaks—by their grayish scaly bark (especially on young specimens) and by their grayish-blue-green leaves. Ranging in age up to about 300 years, these particular thick-trunked Engelmanns have real character. Their multifarious, wandering limbs divide into innumerable branches, and their dense foliage spreads outward to cast black pools of shade upon the ground.

There's much more to see along this little trail than the oaks. Purple needle-grass—a native, fire-resistant and drought-resistant bunchgrass that survives by sending down roots several feet deep—thrives in the meadows. The native grasses growing on the Santa Rosa Plateau, in fact, comprise the largest bunchgrass prairie in Southern California. Prescribed burning is used as a tool here to maintain the native grasses and suppress nonnative, invasive species.

Cole Creek trickles alongside the first part of the trail, its bed sculpted with small ponds (or *tenajas*) that support frogs, pond turtles, and newts. California sycamores twine upward among the oaks. One of these oaks has a hollow interior, providing nesting habitat for birds such as woodpeckers and screech owls.

Trip 2: Santa Rosa Plateau Loop

Distance	7.5 miles
Total Elevation Gain/Loss	650'/650'
Hiking Time	4 hours
Optional Map	USGS 7.5-min *Wildomar*
Best Times	November through May
Agency	SRPER
Difficulty	★★★

For a comprehensive look at the Santa Rosa Plateau Ecological Reserve, try this half-day hike, which will introduce you to virtually every attractive feature characteristic of Southern California's foothills.

Start on the left branch of the Oak Tree self-guiding trail (Trip 1). It takes you through Engelmann oak woodland to the start of the Trans Preserve Trail, located at post 11. Follow the Trans Preserve Trail for 1.7 miles over rolling and sometimes wooded terrain to the Vernal Pool Trail atop Mesa de Colorado. Head left (east) past one of the largest vernal pools in California (39 acres at maximum capacity). The hard-pan surface underneath vernal pools is generally impervious to water, so once filled during winter storms, the pools dry only by evaporation. Unusual and sometimes unique species of flowering plants have evolved around the perimeter of many vernal pools, including this one. As the pool's perimeter contracts during the steadily lengthening and warming days of spring, successive waves of annual wildflowers bloom along the pool's moist margin. By July or August, there's nothing to be seen but a desiccated depression, its barren surface glaring in the hot sun.

Continue east on the Vernal Pool Trail, and descend from Mesa de Colorado toward the two adobe buildings of the former Santa Rosa Ranch. If it's early in the morning, pause on the way down to scan (with binoculars, if you have them) the

On the Trans Preserve Trail

grassy slopes that lie below you in the north. One hiker told me that he has never seen so much wildlife (especially deer) in one place at one time as right here. Survey the skies, too, for patrolling raptors.

At the bottom of the grade, amidst the plentiful shade of live oaks, you'll find Riverside County's oldest known buildings—about 150 years old. If you are tired or hot, you can "bail out" here by making a bee line back to the start via the Lomas Trail. Otherwise, continue on the 7.5-mile route by following the Punta Mesa Trail (a disused road) down across De Luz Creek and back uphill, heading north. At the next intersection, turn left, travel briefly west, and veer right on the aptly named Vista Grande Trail. Upon reaching the crest ahead (elevation 1940 feet), let your gaze take in hundreds of acres of wind-rippled grass, and admire the often snow-dusted peaks of the distant San Bernardino and San Jacinto mountains, in the north and northeast, respectively.

When you reach the Tenaja Truck Trail, turn left and return to the starting point.

2000 Update: The Santa Rosa Plateau Ecological Reserve continues to expand. There is a proposal to add a 2000-acre "wildlife corridor" on the reserve's west side so as to ensure a viable ecological connection between the reserve and San Mateo Wilderness. The trailhead mapped at the sharp bend in Tenaja Road on page 79 has been permanently closed. Hikers may start from the picnic area 0.7 mile mile north of the sharp bend (where a small visitor center is now open on weekends); at the new Hidden Valley trailhead on Tenaja Road just west of the sharp bend; or at the west end of the Vernal Pool Trail. In addition, new trails have been opened in the newly purchased Sylvan Ranch property on the northwest side of the reserve. Trail maps of the entire reserve are available at the visitor center. A small fee is now charged for the use of the reserve.

Stream in Mayhew Canyon

Santa Ana Mountains

Area M-1: Santa Ana Mountains— Main Divide

Most of the higher Santa Ana Mountains—along with their extensions to the southeast and east—the Elsinore and Santa Margarita mountains, lie within the overall boundary of Cleveland National Forest, fixed by Congress in 1908. Today the administrative subunit covering this area is called the Trabuco Ranger District. Of the 255 square miles encompassed by the district, about 210 square miles are managed by the federal government. Private "inholdings" make up the difference.

In this book we divide the Trabuco District into three parts—northern, middle, and southern—because of the distinctly different character of each one. In this section (Area M-1), covering most of what is called the "Main Divide" of the Santa Ana Mountains, visitor facilities are almost nil, but an extensive dirt-road system, along with a few trails, makes it relatively easy for hikers to get around. The middle section (Area M-2) along Ortega Highway has camping facilities, many trails, and good access to them. The southern section (Area M-3), San Mateo Canyon Wilderness, has an extensive trail system that receives varying degrees of maintenance.

Geographically, the Main Divide is an important watershed divide, featuring several of the Santa Ana's highest peaks. These include (from north to south) Sierra Peak; Pleasants Peak; Bedford Peak; Bald Peak; Modjeska and Santiago peaks, together forming the familiar "Old Saddleback"; and Trabuco Peak. These rounded summits (except Modjeska) serve,

in connect-the-dots fashion, as benchmarks for the Orange/Riverside county line.

East of the Main Divide, water flows down steep-cut canyons to Temescal Valley—a sunken trench on the far side of the Elsinore Fault—where it usually percolates into the water table. During times of flood the runoff makes its way north to Corona and joins the Santa Ana River.

West of the divide, water flows down canyons steep in their upper reaches, narrow and rather straight in their midsections, and broad and gently meandering through the foothills. If not claimed by percolation or detained by dams, the water makes its way across Orange County's coastal plain—typically in concrete-lined channels—to the sea.

The Main Divide appears treeless and rather austere from a distance, yet it holds many surprises. The ubiquitous chaparral and sage-scrub cover that appears half-dead in summer's blazing heat turns bright green and pleasingly pungent at the touch of autumn's first steady rain. Early spring sunshine brings forth a profusion of blossoms and perfumelike aromas.

On both sides of the Main Divide, coniferous trees cling to moist pockets of soil, and scattered springs feed perennial and seasonal creeks that in turn sustain willows, sycamores, maples, bay laurels, and centuries-old oaks in the bottoms of the deepest ravines and canyons.

Presently there are no camping facilities in the Main Divide area. A proposed cooperative agreement, however, envisions

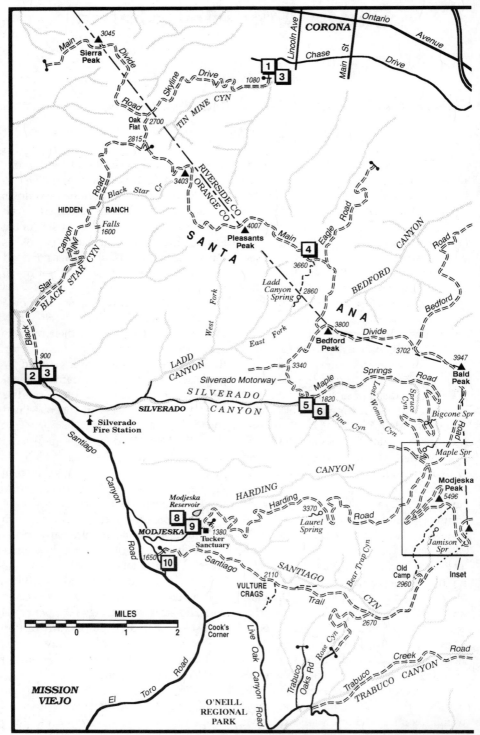

Area M-1: Santa Ana Mountains—Main Divide

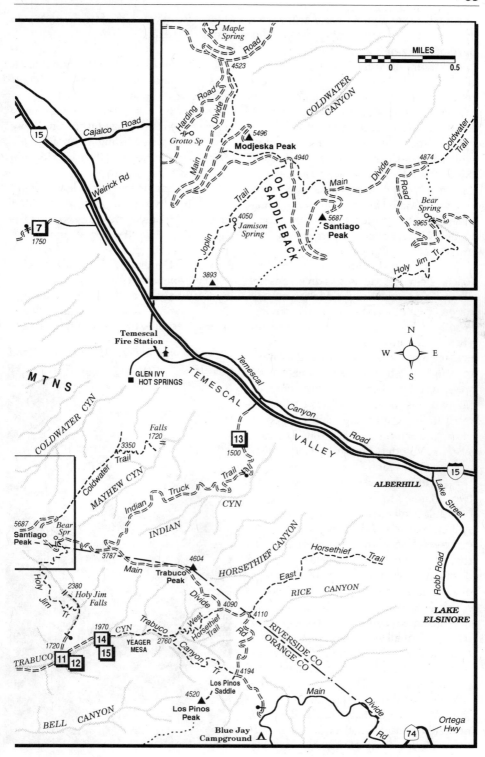

Orange County taking over management of one or more of the westside canyons and developing camping facilities there.

Hikers have the privilege of unrestricted use of all forest roads and trails (except for some that pass through private inholdings—these are posted) unless the Forest Service declares a fire closure during extremely dry weather. Fire closures, which are rare, result in a ban of all use of the forest. At all times and in all seasons "no fires/no camping" is the unbending rule in the Main Divide area—though hiking before dawn and after sunset is not prohibited. No fees or permits are required for use of the Main Divide area.

The Main Divide's extensive dirt-road system, serving uses as diverse as fire control, access to utility and telecommunications facilities, and recreational driving, is both the blessing and the bane of hikers. These wide pathways permit relatively easy passage into some of the Santa Anas' more remote areas, but invite at times use by speeding off-road vehicles and motorcycles. Many hikers themselves drive on them to reach trailheads that are otherwise too remote to reach on foot in a day. The road system also offers remote and often challenging routes for mountain bikers.

With strapped budgets over the past two decades, the Forest Service has not been able to maintain the Main Divide road system year-round. In past years, the first gully-washing storm in autumn closed the roads to public motor-vehicle use for the duration of the rainy season. In April, May, or June, after the ruts were filled and the rockfall cleared, the vehicle gates swung open again. Recently, the Forest Service has tried to normalize the seasonal closures so that they are predictable for users. Currently, the annual seasonal closure (for motor vehicles) is intended to run from November 1 through May 15.

When permitted, motorized travel is normally restricted to the following roads: Main Divide Road (south of Black Star Canyon Road only), Bedford Road, Maple Springs Road, and Indian Truck Trail. Call the Trabuco Ranger District office in Corona (909-736-1811) or visit any national-forest fire station in the Santa Anas for current information on the road system.

In addition to forest roads seasonally or never open to vehicles, hikers can choose among several interesting foot trails in the Main Divide area, especially in the Holy Jim and Trabuco canyon areas.

Trailheads in the west-side canyons of the Main Divide, notably Black Star, Silverado, Modjeska, and Trabuco, offer Orange County urbanites very easy opportunities to get away from it all. The first three are within 45 minutes' drive of Anaheim, Garden Grove, Santa Ana, and other core cities. Ready access is provided by Santiago Canyon and El Toro roads, and then by secondary roads into the canyons themselves.

Frozen mud puddle, Main Divide Road

The east-side trailheads, less than an hour away from central Orange County, are reached by way of the Riverside Free-way (Highway 91) and Interstate 15, which runs through the Temescal Valley at the foot of the Santa Anas.

Trip 1: Sierra Peak via Skyline Drive

Distance	14.5 miles
Total Elevation Gain/Loss	3200'/3200'
Hiking Time	7½ hours
Recommended Map	Cleveland National Forest recreation map
Optional Maps	USGS 7.5-min *Corona South, Black Star Canyon*
Best Times	November through March
Agency	CNF/TD
Difficulty	★★★

Wait for a winter storm to clear the air, then try this viewful hike to Sierra Peak, the rounded promontory anchoring the north end of the Santa Ana Mountains. Because the route follows well-graded ser-vice roads throughout and the climbing is quite gradual, this is an ideal route for en-ergetic runners and mountain bicyclists as well as hikers.

Around the winter solstice, an after-noon/evening trek to and from Sierra Peak can be very rewarding. Plan to reach the peak in time to watch the sun drop into the Pacific (before 5 P.M. from early Novem-ber to early January). Then stroll back down under the stars, arriving at your car before 8 P.M. Nights lit by a full or nearly full moon are best; otherwise the glare of the city lights below makes it hard to see the ground underfoot. Don't forget extra warm clothes and a flashlight.

Geologically, this is an interesting area. About 2 miles up from the trailhead, you'll cross the Elsinore Fault zone, with crumbly 150-million-year-old metavol-canic rock to the southwest and colorfully banded marine sedimentary rocks half that age to the northeast. Near Sierra Peak are some nice exposures of sandstone with embedded cobbles.

To reach the trailhead, take either the Lincoln Avenue or Main Street exit from Freeway 91 in Corona and drive 3 miles south to Chase Drive. Turn west on Chase, then turn left where Skyline Drive branches south. Pull up and park near the massive gate designed to keep vehicles out.

Go through the pedestrian pass-through, and continue up the road. After the first mile, the road swings back away and up from the mouth of Tin Mine Can-yon, formerly an open target-shooting area but now mercifully quiet. Soon views open up of nearby Corona and more distant Riv-erside and San Bernardino, backed up by the towering summits of the San Gabriel and San Bernardino mountains. In the carpetlike orange groves below, new sub-divisions seem to push and leapfrog along.

Oak Flat, 4.8 miles from the gate, is marked by grassland dotted with a few oaks and a radio communications complex. At the road junction turn right (Black Star Canyon Road goes left, south) and con-tinue along the main divide of the Santa Anas toward Sierra Peak, the antenna-bris-tling summit to the north. On top there's a great view of the Chino Hills and Pomona Valley to the north, the broad trough of lower Santa Ana Canyon to the west, and endless miles of L.A. Basin suburbia stretching toward the Pacific Ocean.

Trip 2: Black Star Canyon Falls

Distance	6.6 miles
Total Elevation Gain/Loss	800'/800'
Hiking Time	4 hours (round trip)
Recommended Maps	USGS 7.5-min *Black Star Canyon*; Cleveland National Forest recreation map
Best Times	November through May
Agency	CNF/TD
Difficulty	★★★

Good timing is the key to catching the waterfall in Black Star Canyon at its best. Since only about 3 square miles of drainage area lie behind it, persistent rains are needed to get more than a dribble of water over the fall. Whether the water is flowing or not, though, the canyon bottom itself is delightful to explore any time the weather is mild.

From the well-marked Silverado Canyon/Black Star Canyon turnoff on Santiago Canyon Road, proceed 0.1 mile toward Silverado Canyon, then turn left (north) on Black Star Canyon Road. After 1.1 miles, a sturdy gate, normally closed and locked, blocks further unauthorized vehicle traffic. Park and begin hiking here. Orange County retains the right of way through both private and public lands ahead; simply stay on the road when traversing lands not included under National Forest jurisdiction (as shown on the National Forest map).

After an uninteresting half mile along the dry, open bed of Santiago Creek, the road abruptly turns east into Black Star Canyon. Scattered oaks, sycamores, and willows, and rows of planted eucalyptus trees provide shade as the road meanders gently uphill along the creekbed. The canyon was named after the nearby Black Star Coal Mine (on private land), which was worked briefly more than a century ago during a silver- and coal-mining boom in the Silverado Canyon area. Look for seams of poor-quality coal in the roadcuts you pass.

At 2.5 miles the road doubles back in a hairpin turn to ascend the sage-covered slopes to the north. You've now reached the corner of Section 30, which is part of Cleveland National Forest. It's time to put on long pants and a long-sleeved shirt to do battle with poison oak and other shrubbery up the canyon. About one hour (0.8 mile) of boulder-hopping, bushwhacking, and moderate hands-and-feet scrambling up the trenchlike confines of the canyon will take you to the base of the falls.

Marine sedimentary rocks are in evidence here. Bold outcrops of stratified, buff-colored siltstone rise hundreds of feet above the canyon bottom, giving safe quarter to nesting raptors and other birds. The creek slides around great blocks of conglomerate rock and pools up in shady grottos concealed amid large oak, alder, sycamore, and bay trees.

The semicircular siltstone headwall that forms the falls fairly drips with mosses and maidenhair ferns, if not water. When the flow is great enough, water cascades 50 feet down a polished chute, and also exits through an old mine shaft cut into the headwall about 15 feet above the falls' base.

By backtracking down-canyon about 200 yards, and then thrashing up a steep ravine to the west (thus outflanking some crumbling cliffs), it's possible to reach nearby Black Star Canyon Road at the 1960-foot contour. But it's far easier and safer to return the way you came, making your way down the creekbed over now-familiar obstacles.

Trip 3: North Main Divide Traverse

	Distance	13.0 miles
	Total Elevation Gain/Loss	1950'/2150'
	Hiking Time	6½ hours
	Recommended Maps	USGS 7.5-min *Corona South, Black Star Canyon*; Cleveland National Forest recreation map
	Best Times	November through April
	Agency	CNF/TD
	Difficulty	★★★

Incorporating parts of Trips 1 and 2 above, this trek over the north crest of the Santa Ana Mountains is perfect for in-shape runners, walkers, and mountain bikers. Relatively easy grades, generally smooth dirt and gravel surfaces, and little or no interference from motor vehicles are yours all the way—though the 13-mile distance is far from trivial. The aftermath of heavy rains, however, can prove to be a serious hindrance especially for cyclists. This is no problem on the Skyline Drive side, but Black Star Canyon Road in the vicinity of Hidden Ranch can turn into one big mudhole.

Because of elevation differences, it's a little easier to begin on the east near Corona and end by way of Black Star Canyon in Orange County. After taking care of transportation arrangements, proceed up the moderate but steady incline of Skyline Drive. Only one brief downhill stretch, about 0.3 mile long, interrupts the climb to Oak Flat. As you cross the county line just before reaching Oak Flat, you'll spot the first of the many "Black Star Canyon Road—use at your own risk" signs posted by Orange County.

At 4.8 miles (Oak Flat intersection) turn left (south) and continue uphill toward the next junction, 5.3 miles, where the Main Divide Road forks left. The tumbledown rock houses nearby, labeled "Beeks Place" on the topo map, are surrounded by an unkempt but still-thriving grove of planted trees—natives like Coulter pine, knobcone pine, and Tecate cypress; plus some non-

natives. Not much shade can be found ahead until you reach scattered oaks and sycamores at Hidden Ranch.

From Beeks Place bear right on Black Star Canyon Road and begin the long, winding descent into the grassy bowl occupied by Hidden Ranch. This privately owned section within national-forest boundaries (Section 19) is a working cattle ranch, truly hidden from the sights and sounds of the city below. Hidden Ranch is quite famous for its human history as well. Bedrock mortars here tell of its use as a major Indian village. It was also the site of an 1831 raid on Indian horse thieves, and the site of a celebrated murder in 1899. While passing through Hidden Ranch you are not allowed to stray from the road.

Past Hidden Ranch, Black Star Canyon Road continues its leisurely descent down some sun-blasted, sage-covered slopes. At 8.7 miles the road swings close to the gorge concealing Black Star Canyon falls. Finally, at 10.5 miles, you reach the cool bottom of Black Star Canyon, and the remaining miles are pleasantly shaded.

Bush poppy on Main Divide Road

Trip 4: Ladd Canyon Spring

Distance	1.8 miles
Total Elevation Gain/Loss	800'/800'
Hiking Time	2 hours (round trip)
Recommended Map	USGS 7.5-min *Corona South*
Best Times	October; May
Agency	CNF/TD
Difficulty	★★

A short jaunt off the Main Divide Road, Ladd Canyon Spring is concealed in a dense grove of live oaks and sycamores near the head of one of the Santa Anas' many westside drainages. Contributing to the beauty are vinelike growths of poison oak twisting upward along the tree trunks, and ferns and wild blackberry vines mantling the shady slopes.

The hike to the spring is a reasonably easy one only when the interior forest roads of the Santa Anas are open to vehicles—normally mid-May through the end of October. With a sturdy vehicle, you can then drive to the head of Ladd Canyon's East Fork via Main Divide Road. When the road system is gated, November through mid-May, you face an additional 10 miles of round-trip hiking via Silverado Motorway from the nearest forest gate in Silverado Canyon.

The starting point is located at a small saddle on Main Divide Road, 0.5 mile west of the signed Eagle Road junction. Park next to an old fenced guzzler (a water catchment facility for wildlife). Back near the Eagle Road junction is a newer and much larger asphalt catchment area designed to gather and store rainwater for firefighting. On clear days the view from here, straight down Bedford Canyon, is stupendous, with Lake Mathews mirroring the distant summit of San Gorgonio Mountain.

The trail to Ladd Canyon Spring is an old, disused jeep road, washed out in several places and partly overgrown by three varieties of aromatic plants: California sagebrush, black sage, and white sage.

Catalina Island from Silverado Motorway

Indian hunters rubbed themselves with sage in order to disguise their scent from game animals; you'll unavoidably do the same by having to push your way through all the vegetation encroaching on this trail.

After descending almost one mile, the old roadbed comes close to the tree-shaded bottom of Ladd Canyon. Drop down through the trees, taking care to step around the poison oak. The spring, a mere seep most of the year, is of somewhat trivial interest, but the cool, sun-dappled ambience of the place makes the hike worthwhile.

Trip 5: Silverado Motorway to Bedford Peak

Distance	6.6 miles
Total Elevation Gain/Loss	2200'/2200'
Hiking Time	4 hours (round trip)
Recommended Maps	USGS 7.5-min *Santiago Peak, Corona South*; or Cleveland National Forest recreation map
Best Times	October through May
Agency	CNF/TD
Difficulty	★★★

This no-nonsense climb to one of the principal summits of the Main Divide is physically demanding enough to serve as an excellent conditioning hike, and scenically rewarding as well. From the west-side trailheads there's no faster way to reach the Main Divide crest by foot.

From Santiago Canyon Road, drive east up Silverado Canyon Road. You'll pass the sites of Carbondale and Silverado, boom towns that popped up in response to coal and silver strikes in the late 1870s. After population in the area peaked at around a thousand, boom turned to bust by 1883 as the nearby coal ledges and silver-ore bodies were depleted. Today, people have returned in force: Silverado Canyon Road is lined with attractive homes and cabins.

After 5.4 miles you arrive at a vehicle turnaround and parking area at the edge of Cleveland National Forest. A plaque here tells of Canada de la Madera ("Timber Canyon"), the original name of the canyon. The upper reaches once yielded pine timber used for joists in the lowland adobes.

On foot now, continue up-canyon past the vehicle gate. In about 300 yards, just after crossing the alder-shaded bottom of the canyon, turn sharply to the left (west) on an unsigned road that climbs sharply up the north wall of the canyon. This is the Silverado Motorway, built originally for fire control, then used for a while by 4-wheel-drive enthusiasts. It is now severely eroded and impassable to motor vehicles.

An excellent view of the whole of Silverado Canyon unfolds as you swing around several hairpin turns. In the road

Bedford Canyon Formation

cuts, a well-stratified, often sharply folded metasedimentary rock (the Bedford Canyon Formation) is exposed. The sediments making up these rocks were deposited on the sea floor more than 150 million years ago, buried and metamorphosed by heat and pressure, and finally elevated to their present position high above sea level.

The road bed stays fairly open and clear until a sharp bend at 1.7 miles (3140 feet), where small landslides have spilled into the road. Weeds and grass underfoot are a nuisance for the next 0.3 mile. At the end of this stretch, an intersection is reached on the shoulder of a ridge overlooking Ladd Canyon to the northwest.

From here follow a wide, graded road northeast along the ridgeline toward Main Divide Road. On reaching Main Divide Road (2.9 miles from the start), turn right, continue 0.3 mile, then walk up the rounded 3800-foot summit of Bedford Peak on the right. There's no place to rest comfortably on the open summit, but the view—from the Pacific coast to the peaks of the Peninsular Ranges—can be stupendous on a clear day.

Trip 6: Silverado-Modjeska Peak Loop

Distance	18.3 miles (to Modjeska Peak and back)
Total Elevation Gain/Loss	4440'/4440'
Hiking Time	9 hours
Recommended Maps	USGS 7.5-min *Santiago Peak, Corona South*; or Cleveland National Forest recreation map
Best Times	November through May
Agency	CNF/TD
Difficulty	★★★★

The goal of this hike, looping up and over the Main Divide, is to reach the summit of Modjeska Peak—the lower, north summit of Old Saddleback. If you omit the out-and-back leg to the peak itself, however, you shorten the trip by 2.5 miles. Either way, this is an all-day trek on foot. During the clear, crisp weather characteristic of certain periods from November through March, this hike can be among the most rewarding and peaceful in southern California.

As in Trip 5, start at the terminus of Silverado Canyon Road and climb to Main Divide Road via Silverado Motorway. Turn south past Bedford Peak and follow Main Divide Road for several undulating miles, passing several small summits along the way. Just north of Bald Peak, a big powerline barely clears the ridge. This 500-kilovolt line, completed in 1987, links the Palm Springs area and Orange County.

There are clear lines of sight in most directions, and most of southern California's highest mountain ranges are in view. Below and to the west, a scant mile away, you can trace the zigzag path of the Maple Springs Road (your return route) across a sparsely timbered slope and down to the bottom of upper Silverado Canyon.

After 8.7 miles (from the start) Main Divide Road comes to an intersection north of, and about 1000 vertical feet below, imposing Modjeska Peak. Swing left, staying on Main Divide Road, and continue 75 yards. Then, turn onto the narrow trail that angles steeply up the road cut on the left, and continue climbing across a slope. After a half mile, you plunge into the shade of some tall chaparral shrubs and small oak trees. After another 0.3 mile you reach the access road leading to Modjeska Peak. Go left and continue 0.5 mile to Modjeska's open summit. On a clear day, the 360°-view of the surrounding mountains, basins, and ocean is obstructed only slightly by the antenna-bristling summit of Santiago Peak, one mile southeast.

Your return to the starting point is now entirely downhill. Retrace your steps to Main Divide Road and continue north to the next road intersection (4523'), and turn left on Maple Springs Road. As you start down, keep right at the next two road intersections so as to stay on Maple Springs Road.

The next several miles on Maple Springs Road are a botanist's delight. On the upper slopes huge Coulter pines soar above thick carpets of manzanita shrubs. Big-cone Douglas-fir, bigleaf maple, bay, and live oak trees crowd together in the larger ravines, casting dense pools of shade

over trickling streams.

On the sixth sharp hairpin turn from the top, 4 miles down from Main Divide Road, you finally reach the bottom of Silverado Canyon. During the last 3 miles, the stream flows merrily along next to the road, flanked by sycamores, alders, and more maples. In spring, California poppy and golden yarrow brighten the roadside, while the celebrated snowy-white Matilija poppy, the "queen of the California wild-flowers," blooms atop swaying stems taller than a man.

Midway down the final stretch is the mouth of Lost Woman Canyon, a tributary draining into Silverado Canyon from the south. When the wind whistles down this canyon, so the old-timers say, it evokes the plaintive sounds of a woman calling for help. Treading softly down the road, mildly hallucinating after many long miles, you may hear her.

Trip 7: Bedford Road

	Distance	8.0 miles (to Main Divide and back)
	Total Elevation Gain/Loss	2300'/2300'
	Hiking Time	4½ hours (round trip)
	Optional Maps	USGS 7.5-min *Corona South*; Cleveland National Forest recreation map
	Best Times	November through April
	Agency	CNF/TD
	Difficulty	★★★

Bedford Road offers hikers the fastest and easiest access to the Main Divide from the east, or Temescal Valley, side. Much of the area south of Bedford Road was swept by the 13,000-acre Silverado Fire of August 1987. Yet just 10 weeks later, in response to early rains, the ashen slopes were covered by an instant crop of verdant grasses. Now there's little hint that a fire burned here in 1987.

High-clearance vehicles should have

no trouble negotiating the always-open lower stretch of Bedford Road leading to the vehicle gate. Exit Interstate 15 at Weirick Road, then proceed south on the west-side frontage road for exactly 0.5 mile. Here turn right (west) on unmarked Bedford Road, which is paved for a while, then dirt thereafter. Drive uphill for 2.1 miles to the vehicle gate, where limited parking space is available at a wide spot in the road.

Coulter pine forest along Maple Springs Road

Except for a half-dozen brief flat or downhill stretches, you'll be gaining elevation steadily as you walk. The road winds up along a ridge affording panoramic views of several Main Divide peaks just ahead, as well as vistas of the distant San Bernardino and San Jacinto mountains to the north and east. In early spring, the shaggy hills all around you turn a bright shade of green. They seem to tumble, like the advancing foamy front of a wave frozen in mid-break, into the broad trench of Temescal Valley below.

Beyond 3.0 miles, bush poppy grows in abundance. At 3.6 miles you'll cross a small flat with a couple of bay trees—possibly planted, since bay trees normally inhabit moist canyons in the Santa Anas. On warm days, this is the place to stop for shade. Upon reaching Main Divide Road (3.9 miles), hike south about 0.1 mile farther to the top of a small knoll where the Forest Service has installed some water-collection devices for fighting fires. Here a slice of the ocean and Orange County's coastal plain is visible on clear days. Bald Peak, about one mile south and a little higher, offers a somewhat better view.

By going west along Main Divide Road past Bedford Peak, then down the Silverado Motorway to the Silverado Canyon roadhead, it's possible to complete a relatively easy, east-west traverse of the Santa Ana Mountain crest, only 9.5 miles long.

Trip 8: Harding Road to Laurel Spring

Distance	10.0 miles
Total Elevation Gain/Loss	2300'/2300'
Hiking Time	5½ hours (round trip)
Optional Maps	USGS 7.5-min *Santiago Peak*; Cleveland National Forest recreation map
Best Times	October through May
Agency	CNF/TD
Difficulty	★★★

Tucked into an upper tributary of Santiago Canyon, Laurel Spring is a lofty mini-retreat just 3 air-miles from the expanding edge of Orange County's outer suburbs. While the surface flow at the spring merely fills a cement watering trough, the abundant groundwater nourishes a thriving thicket of California bay (bay laurel) trees. Under the cathedral-like canopy of these trees, the cool, pungent odor of bay leaves wafts on the breeze like incense.

The long walk up to the spring on Harding Road is relieved—in the cooler, wetter months, at least—by the pleasure of the aromatic and sometimes colorful sage-scrub and chaparral vegetation. In spring, blue-flowering ceanothus and matilija poppies put on a great show. Harding Road (formerly called Harding Truck Trail) is passable for fire trucks, but normally closed to motorized traffic, with gates at both bottom (Modjeska Canyon) and top (Main Divide Road).

Early risers will appreciate this hike, especially in fall and early winter, when late sunrises make it convenient to hit the trail in time to enjoy a bit of stargazing before dawn's first light. Before the sun cleared the horizon one November morning, I ran into two other groups of hikers on the Harding Road with just that idea in mind.

To reach the trailhead, take either Modjeska Canyon Road or Modjeska Grade Road from Santiago Canyon Road into the rustic canyon community of Modjeska. Here Santiago Creek threads a course through Modjeska Canyon, the name given to a short stretch of the gorge that more logically bears the name "Santiago Canyon" east (upstream) of here. The ubiquitous place name "Modjeska" honors famed 19th-century Shakespearean actress Helena Modjeska, whose 400-acre "Forest of Arden" retreat was located hereabouts.

Near the east end of Modjeska Canyon Road, a large wooden sign identifies Tucker Wildlife Sanctuary, a small biological study area operated by the Fullerton campus of California State University. The intermixing of chaparral, sage scrub, oak woodland, and riparian habitats here attracts nearly two hundred species of birds and animals over the various seasons of the year. After hiking on Harding Road, you can visit the sanctuary: take a guided tour, visit the wildlife museum, or simply unwind by relaxing under the oak trees. Hours are 9 A.M. to 4 P.M. daily.

Parking space is scarce in Modjeska. For the purpose of hiking Harding Road, you should park in the large gravel lot next to the small observatory dome at the east end of the sanctuary. Cross the paved road, and walk up the dirt road signed "5S08." This is Harding Road. Immediately on your right is the 0.1-mile Chaparral Nature Trail loop, part of the wildlife sanctuary. Past the sturdy vehicle gate, you wind a little higher past a "no camping/no fires" sign posted at the boundary of the national forest. Ahead is a bold outcrop of conglomerate rock, consisting of sediments laid down in a marine environment roughly 80 million years ago. More of this erosion-resistant, cliff-forming layer will be seen on ridges to the north and south as you climb a little higher.

At a road fork in 0.4 mile, stay right; the left road goes down to the off-limits Modjeska Reservoir in Harding Canyon. At 0.7 mile a ridgetop clearing next to a hairpin turn provides a view straight up the tree-choked bottom of Harding Canyon, a tributary of Santiago Canyon. The upper reaches of this seemingly impenetrable canyon were the scene of a short-lived mining boomlet shortly following the bigger boom in Silverado Canyon. In 1878 a pair of prospectors discovered some nodules containing lead and silver ore about 3 miles up from the present-day reservoir. Soon miners swarmed so thickly throughout the canyon that, according to a newspaper account of the day, a man could hardly swing a pick without "perforating his neighbor."

After 1.0 mile Harding Road descends about 100 feet (the only reversal in the steady ascent to Laurel Spring) in order to edge around a couple of steep ravines. Climbing again, you round the nose of a ridge and come upon (1.6 miles) the remnants of a wooden structure—known as the "goat shed" by local residents—overlooking the whole of Modjeska Canyon. To the east, a trench-like section of Santiago Canyon winds upward toward Old Saddleback.

The road continues generally east on or near the ridgeline dividing Harding and Santiago canyons. In early morning, the view behind is often that of cottony layers of fog or low clouds obscuring the coastal plain. The hum of traffic in the distant suburbs penetrates the murk.

At 4.9 miles a large landslide lies on the left. Just beyond, the road bends around the head of a ravine densely choked with bay laurel. On the right, look for the steep, narrow pathway that leads down about 50 vertical feet to Laurel Spring.

Trip 9: Harding Road to Main Divide

Distance	19.0 miles
Total Elevation Gain/Loss	3650'/3650'
Hiking Time	9 hours (round trip)
Optional Maps	USGS 7.5-min *Santiago Peak*; Cleveland National Forest recreation map
Best Times	November through March
Agency	CNF/TD
Difficulty	★★★★

This challenging cool-weather trip is ideal for the exercise-minded, be they long-distance hikers, mountain runners, or mountain bicyclists. Since well over half this route stays on the north side of the ridgeline dividing Santiago and Harding canyons, the long shadows of late fall and winter provide plenty of welcome shade. There is also the distinct possibility of skiing the upper part of Harding Road immediately following a cold, wet winter storm. (You would, of course, have to carry your cross-country skis perhaps 3 or more miles up the road to the first snow.)

Begin as in Trip 8 above. If you drop down from Harding Road to visit Laurel Spring (5.0 miles), you can get back to the road a little faster by following a 0.2-mile-long path that curls south and east from the spring and joins the road again.

At 6.0 miles Harding Road curls over to the north-facing side of the ridgeline and thereafter sticks to the slopes overlooking Harding Canyon. Dense chaparral—manzanita, scrub oak, mountain mahogany, and blue-flowering ceanothus (wild lilac)—mantles these slopes, but some Coulter pines and canyon live oaks rise above the shrubbery. In protected pockets both north and south of the road, small clusters of battered big-cone Douglas-firs have found a safe haven from the fires that periodically sweep through. In the larger, north-draining ravines, where moisture is retained in the soil, a smattering of small willows and

sycamores is also seen.

Grotto Spring, at 8.6 miles, is normally completely dry. At 9.5 miles you reach Main Divide Road at a saddle overlooking the big drainage to the north—upper Silverado Canyon.

Options for further exploration include climbing Modjeska and Santiago peaks, which lie 1.3 miles and 2.4 miles away, respectively, via the shortest routes. Mountain cyclists can piece together a superb 27-mile ride by stringing together Harding and Maple Springs roads, then closing the loop via the paved Silverado Canyon, Santiago Canyon, and Modjeska Canyon roads.

In Santiago Canyon

Trip 10: Santiago Trail

Distance	15.0 miles (to Old Camp and back)
Total Elevation Gain/Loss	2650'/2650'
Hiking Time	8 hours (round trip)
Recommended Maps	USGS 7.5-min *El Toro, Santiago Peak*; or Cleveland National Forest recreation map
Best Times	November through April
Agency	CNF/TD
Difficulty	★★★

Yesteryear, Old Camp was a popular rendezvous point for hunting parties using the Joplin Trail between Rose Canyon and Old Saddleback. Now only remnants of the Joplin Trail remain, and Old Camp is simply a flat spot in Santiago Canyon shaded by massive live oaks, bay laurels, and bigleaf maples.

Old Camp retains its charm as a remote hideaway. It's well-worth the daylong hike if the weather is cool. In late fall the maples really put on a show, and by winter or early spring the adjoining creek, screened by alders, bubbles with a delightfully pure flow of water.

Today Old Camp is reached by way of the Santiago Trail, a fire road closed to motor vehicles. Sticking close to the original Joplin route over part of its length, it runs for about 7 miles along the sunny ridgeline just south of Santiago Canyon, finally dropping abruptly into the canyon. The walk can be tedious at times, but there are diversions for the adventurous. At least four primitive pathways descend into the depths of Santiago Canyon from points along the way, offering a taste of a moist, green, almost gloomy environment totally unlike the sunstruck one on the ridgeline.

The most popular starting place is along Modjeska Grade Road (the southern of the two roads leading to the community of Modjeska) at a point 0.5 mile north of Santiago Canyon Road. Here the roadway tops a saddle, and the Santiago Trail, blocked by a steel gate, strikes off to the

east. Park off the pavement, taking care not to block the gate. Normally the first mile of trail is open to hikers, even though it crosses a piece of undeveloped private land before it enters Cleveland National Forest.

The hike on Santiago Trail is uneventful until you begin skirting the back side of the Vulture Crags (2.8 miles). These broken outcrops of conglomerate rock served as a nesting site for California condors over a hundred years ago. In a little while you can look back and note, below the crags, layer upon layer of beige to brick-red marine sediments, all spectacularly tilted as a result of the rise of the Santa Ana Mountain crest to the east.

At 3.7 miles the Santiago Trail makes a bend at the 2400-foot contour, and a narrow, partially overgrown trail strikes off obliquely down the slope. This is the easiest and safest way to reach the canyon bottom short of Old Camp. In late fall a phantasmagoric pattern of bright maple leaves carpets the stream banks and limpid pools, and newly unfurled ferns adorn the lower slopes. Downstream, you can find evidence of mining (circa 1880) in the form of scattered bricks, cast-iron machine parts, prospect holes, and tailings mostly well hidden among the leaf litter and dense vegetation. Wear long pants if you poke around here: you'll probably run into some poison oak and scratchy chaparral. There's an active mining claim down in this part of the canyon, so be sure to respect the rights of the claim holder. Also remember that the old mining debris is considered historic and therefore legally protected against removal.

After 7.2 miles on the Santiago Trail, the road forks. A short spur road continues upward to follow a small powerline, while the Santiago Trail bears left and descends to Old Camp (7.5 miles). In addition to the variety of trees already mentioned, you'll find growths of wild blackberry, buckthorn ceanothus, redberry, coffee berry, and bracken fern in the area.

Further exploration in the area might proceed along the following lines: With the aid of the *Santiago Peak* topo map, it's possible to follow the upper part of the Joplin Trail as far as the low point (between Modjeska and Santiago peaks) in Old Saddleback. From Old Camp the trail

threads through a shady tributary of Santiago Canyon, then gains a brush-covered slope, passing west of a 3893-foot knob. After winding amid some oaks, it angles up a steep slope thickly covered by chamise and buckthorn, a prickly variety of ceanothus. At about 1.3 miles from Old Camp, the trail descends a little, passes through a beautiful thicket of live oaks, bay laurels, and bigcone Douglas-fir, and returns to the bed of Santiago Canyon about 100 yards above Jamison Spring. Another 0.7 mile of ascent brings you to Main Divide Road atop the saddle.

The Joplin Trail is lightly maintained and therefore may be difficult to follow. In recent years hardy mountain bikers have discovered it, and this in itself has contributed to keeping it minimally clear of encroaching brush.

Trip 11: Holy Jim Falls

Distance	2.8 miles
Total Elevation Gain/Loss	650'/650'
Hiking Time	1½ hours (round trip)
Optional Map	USGS 7.5-min *Santiago Peak*
Best Times	November through June
Agency	CNF/TD
Difficulty	★★

Sometimes the intimacy of a tiny, hidden waterfall is more aesthetically rewarding than the thunder of a famous one. Such is the case with Holy Jim Falls. Tucked into a short, steep canyon draining the southeast flank of Santiago Peak, the falls are seemingly remote but relatively easily reached on foot. The last stretch of trail leading to the falls may be a little overgrown with poison oak, so wear long pants and a long-sleeved shirt.

The drive up Trabuco Canyon to the trailhead is an adventure in itself, not one to be undertaken by low-slung autos. Rocks and potholes are the norm. Most standard passengers cars will do fine if driven slowly.

From a point just south of where the paved Trabuco Canyon Road fords the dry wash of Arroyo Trabuco, turn east on unsigned, dirt-surfaced Trabuco Creek Road. Proceed 4.7 miles, taking care not to blunder up someone's dirt driveway. Many cabins (on leased Forest Service land) are passed along the way, some tucked away in beautiful groves of oaks and sycamores.

The remnants of some rather unproductive tin prospects lie on the slopes to the left about 4 miles up Trabuco Canyon. This is one of the few places where tin has been mined in the United States. Another mine, west of Lake Mathews on the far side of the Santa Anas, produced a more significant quantity—enough ore to yield about 130 tons of tin metal.

After 4.7 miles you'll come to a dirt parking area on the left. Park here and continue on foot, walking up the road that branches north up along the east bank of the stream in Holy Jim Canyon. More cabins under the sheltering trees are passed before you reach, 0.5 mile up-canyon, a sturdy steel gate.

A century ago this canyon was home to settlers who eked out a living by raising bees. One beekeeper, James T. Smith, became so famous for his cursing habit that he was popularly named "Cussin' Jim." Other nicknames bestowed on him included "Lyin' Smith," "Greasy Jim," and "Salvation Smith." Dignified government cartographers invented a new one, "Holy Jim."

Beyond the gate a narrow trail continues upstream, crossing the creek seven times in 0.7 mile. The usual native trees, ferns, and chaparral shrubs line the canyon, but you'll also see naturalized fig trees and a purple-flowered ground cover called vinca (or periwinkle), the latter two introduced by the early settlers. Just after the last stream crossing, the trail switches back sharply to the left and begins ascending the

Holy Jim Falls

west slope of the canyon. Leave the main trail at this point and continue straight up the bottom of the canyon on an even narrower trail. After about 400 yards you'll come to the shallow pool and grotto at the base of the falls. Above it the water cascades perhaps 18 feet over a broken cliff.

Trip 12: Santiago Peak via Holy Jim Trail

Distance	15.0 miles
Total Elevation Gain/Loss	3950'/3950'
Hiking Time	9 hours (round trip)
Recommended Map	USGS 7.5-min *Santiago Peak*
Best Times	November through April
Agency	CNF/TD
Difficulty	★★★★

To the Indians, it was *Kalawpa* ("a wooded place"), the lofty resting place of the deity Chiningchinish. Early settlers and surveyors named it variously Mount

Downey, Trabuco Peak, Temescal Mountain, and Santiago Peak. Finally, mapmakers decided on the name that eventually stuck: Santiago. Today's 'dozer-scraped summit overrun with telecommunications antennae hardly pays just homage to the peak's historic and scenic values. Witness, for example, this record of its first documented ascent in 1853, by a group of lawmen pursuing horse thieves up Coldwater Canyon:

> After an infinite amount of scrambling, danger and hard labor, we stood on the very summit of the Temescal mountain, now by some called Santiago... where we beheld with pleasure a sublime view, more than worth the journey and ascent ...

In 1861, while making a geologic survey of the Santa Anas, William Brewer and Josiah Whitney reached the same summit on their second try, using the ridge north of Coldwater Canyon. Their impressions echoed the sentiments of the earlier climbers: "The view more than repaid us for all we had endured."

The view so enthusiastically described by these early climbers is equally spectacular today—given, perhaps, a clearer-than-average winter day. Under good conditions, you can trace the coastline from Point Loma to Point Dume, spot both Santa Catalina Island and San Clemente Island, and scratch your head trying to identify the plethora of mountain ranges and lesser promontories filling the landscape inland.

Clockwise around the compass from northwest to southeast the major ranges on the horizon are the Santa Monica, San Gabriel, San Bernardino, Little San Bernardino, San Jacinto, Santa Rosa, Palomar, and Cuyamaca mountains. To the south you might see several of the lower ranges along the Mexican border and perhaps glimpse the flat-topped summit of Table Mountain,

a few miles inland from the Baja California coast. In the west and northwest, smog permitting, the flat urban tapestry spreads outward, spiked by the glass skyscrapers of downtown Los Angeles.

Don't underestimate the time required to bag Santiago Peak by way of the Holy Jim Trail. In winter, you'll need an early start to ensure a daylight return. With summit temperatures roughly 20 degrees cooler than below, you should pack along some extra clothing. Plenty of water is a good idea too: Bear Spring, on the way to the summit, should not be considered a potable source.

Begin this hike as in Trip 11 above, but continue following the main trail as it switchbacks up the chaparral-covered west wall of Holy Jim Canyon. Well traveled but minimally cleared of encroaching vegetation, the trail offers intimate glimpses of the immediate surroundings flashing by at eyeball level. Unlike walking on wide fire roads, there is a sense of motion and accomplishment as you ascend this trail.

Soon a few antenna structures atop Santiago Peak come into view, tantalizingly close, but about 3000 feet higher. At 2.7 miles, the trail crosses the bed of Holy Jim Canyon at elevation 3480 feet, well above the falls. You may be tempted at this point to follow the line of scattered trees that struggle up toward the head of the canyon, or try another short cut to the summit by way of the scree-covered slopes left or right; however, loose rock and thickets of thorny ceanothus would surely cost you more time, effort, and grief than you ever imagined.

So continue ahead on the trail, where soon you make a delicate traverse over a landslide. After another mile on sunny, south-facing slopes, you contour around a ridge and suddenly enter a dark and shady recess filled with oaks, sycamores, bigleaf maples and big-cone Douglas-firs. By 4.5 miles, you come to Main Divide Road, opposite Bear Spring.

An old, overgrown, short-cut trail behind Bear Spring might take you up a little more quickly, but it's easier and more pleasant to stick to Main Divide Road from now on. Three more miles of steady climbing in sun and in shade bring you to Santiago's summit.

An observation platform, offering the only means of getting a 360° view, is shielded by a formidable fence, so you must walk around the summit area to take in the complete panorama. Modjeska Peak, one mile northwest and about 200 feet lower, isn't high enough to block the view of any far-horizon features.

The fine-grained rock covering both summits of Old Saddleback is the prototype of the "Santiago Peak Volcanics" exposed on many of the coastal mountain ranges extending south through San Diego County into Baja California. These metamorphosed volcanic-rock formations were originally part of a chain of volcanic islands that collided with our continent some 80 million years ago.

Falls in Mayhew Canyon

Trip 13: Indian Truck Trail

Distance	13.2 miles (to Main Divide and back)
Total Elevation Gain/Loss	2500'/2500'
Hiking Time	6½ hours (round trip)
Optional Maps	USGS 7.5-min *Alberhill, Santiago Peak*; Cleveland National Forest recreation map
Best Times	November through April
Agency	CNF/TD
Difficulty	★★★

The most pleasant, if not the shortest, way to hike to the main divide from the east is by way of Indian Truck Trail ("Indian Road" on some maps). Maintained as a high-standard, one-lane dirt road seasonally open to motor-vehicle traffic, it features easy grades throughout, intermittent shade during the fall and winter months, and nice views because of its predominately ridgetop alignment. Hikers and mountain bikers have it all to themselves during the usual rainy-season motor-vehicle closures.

Trivial as a traffic artery, the Indian Truck Trail nevertheless merits its own full interchange with Interstate 15. From the end of the southbound exit ramp, drive 0.35 mile west (past the end of the pavement) to a road fork. Turn left here and continue another 0.9 mile to a second road fork: here a private road into a Korean church camp bears left, and the Indian Truck Trail bears right. A vehicle gate lies ahead, but parking is very limited there, so you should probably try to park short of the second fork.

Indian Truck Trail starts making an earnest ascent just past the church camp. After running 3 miles along the divide between Indian and Mayhew canyons, Indian Truck Trail makes a decided switch from the hot south side to the cool north side of the ridge. Ferns grow in profusion along the shady road cuts, and the spreading limbs of live oaks and big-cone Douglas-firs frame a beautiful view of the Temescal Valley and the San Bernardino Mountains.

To the north a mile away, you may spot some switchbacks on the steep slope north of Mayhew Canyon. These belong to a newer alignment of the Coldwater Trail, which (if it is ever extended as planned) will cross Mayhew Canyon and connect with Indian Truck Trail. Hidden in Mayhew Canyon's depths is one of the purest streams in the Santa Anas, with Eden-like groves of live oak, sycamore, bigleaf maple, big-cone Douglas-fir, alder and cottonwood; spectacular wildflowers such as the matilija poppy and tiger lily; and a sublime set of falls. Alas, there's no public access from the canyon's mouth, and any other way in involves serious bushwhacking.

After about 5 miles, Indian Truck Trail traverses somewhat drier slopes, mantled with dense growths of manzanita and ceanothus and dotted with Coulter pines. In the final two switchback legs, the road climbs to a saddle, joining (at 6.6 miles) Main Divide Road. Here you can look southwest toward the hills of southern Orange County and the coastline. On clear winter afternoons the glimmer of sunlight on the ocean's surface is breathtaking.

Indian Truck Trail, the Holy Jim Trail (Trip 12), and a short piece of Main Divide Road together make up an excellent transmountain route. Total distance is 12.5 miles from the parking area at the junction of Holy Jim and Trabuco canyons to the bottom of the Indian Truck Trail grade.

Trip 14: Trabuco Canyon

Distance	3.6 miles
Total Elevation Gain/Loss	850' / 850'
Hiking Time	1½ hours (round trip)
Optional Maps	USGS 7.5-min *Santiago Peak, Alberhill*
Best Times	October through June
Agency	CNF/TD
Difficulty	★★

Starting from the east terminus of Trabuco Creek Road, an old truck road turned narrow footpath meanders up to some of the most idyllic spots in the Santa Anas. Upper Trabuco Canyon is home to Orange County's biggest alder grove; to fine specimens of live oak, bay laurel, and maple; to a tiny community of madrones;

and to a wide variety of spectacular spring wildflowers. Historically, the canyon is significant for its mining activity, and as the site of the killing of Southern California's last wild grizzly bear in 1908.

To reach the trailhead, you must navigate up 5.7 miles of poorly maintained dirt road, a job for autos with high clearance and sturdy shock absorbers (see Trip 11 above for more details). Beyond the cluster of cabins at the mouth of Holy Jim Canyon, continue east one mile to a small turnaround with parking for perhaps four or five cars.

From here the trail passes under some large oaks, runs along the creekbed for a stretch, and then decidedly sticks to the sunny slope north of the creek. This slope is botanically best in late March and April, sporting colorful displays of bush lupine, matilija poppy, paintbrush, wild sweet pea, red and sticky monkeyflowers,

prickly phlox, Mariposa lily, wild hyacinth, penstemon, and other spring flowers.

After 1.0 mile the trail passes close to an old adit, one of several reminders of gold-and-silver-mining activity, which persisted until about 1925. Some scraggly bigcone Douglas-fir trees can be seen on a darkly vegetated slope to the south, part of a small, privately owned inholding in the National Forest which includes Yaeger Mesa. Early miner Jake Yaeger built his cabin in the shade of a spreading maple down near the creek.

At 1.8 miles you come to the signed junction of the Horsethief Trail, half-concealed in thickets of brush and poison oak. Down below, the alder-shaded creekbed is a fine place to picnic or rest before heading back along the same trail. Read on for a description of an extended loop hike circling the head of Trabuco Canyon.

Trip 15: West Horsethief-Trabuco Canyon Loop

Distance	10.0 miles
Total Elevation Gain/Loss	2700'/2700'
Hiking Time	6 hours
Recommended Maps	USGS 7.5-min *Santiago Peak, Alberhill*
Best Times	November through April
Agency	CNF/TD
Difficulty	★★★

The combination of wide-open views atop the Main Divide, and passages through pockets of dense chaparral and timber in the uppermost reaches of Trabuco Canyon make this one of the more varied and interesting hikes in this book. Depending on the level of maintenance the trails receive, there may be passages overgrown by brush and poison oak. Wear long pants, or at least have them handy in your pack.

You begin, as in Trip 14, with a steady climb 1.8 miles up Trabuco Canyon to a junction, with the West Horsethief Trail

branching left. Take it. Earlier, you probably spotted switchbacks carving up the treeless slope that now lies east of you. These replaced the original straight-up-the-ridge route used by Indians in prehistoric times and by horse thieves in the Spanish days. Traffic by hikers and mountain bikers in recent years has helped keep today's trail clear of encroaching vegetation. Nonetheless, some sections are very rough and rocky. After following a canyon bottom for a short while, the West Horsethief Trail begins climbing in earnest, zigzagging through dense chaparral. During the coolness of the morning, diligent effort will get you to the top of this tedious stretch fast enough; later in the day this could be a hot, energy-sapping climb.

After 1100 feet of elevation gain the trail straightens, begins to level out along a ridge, and enters a vegetation zone dominated by manzanita and blue-flowering ceanothus. Cool "mountain" air washes over you, perhaps bearing the scent of the pines that lie ahead. Nearly coincident with the change of vegetation is a change in the rocks and soils underfoot. As you climb higher, light-colored granitic boulders and soil replace the dark-brown, crumbly metasedimentary rocks seen earlier. Although the younger granitic rock doesn't crop out below, you may remember having seen granitic boulders down in the bed of Trabuco Canyon. These resistant blocks, originally weathered out of the granitic mass above, were swept downhill during flash floods.

At 3.3 miles from the Trabuco Canyon roadhead, the Horsethief Trail joins

The Trabuco Canyon Trail

Main Divide Road in a sparse grove of Coulter pines. Turn right and follow the road east, then south, for an easy, meandering, viewful 2.5 miles. On the left you will soon pass the East Horsethief Trail, currently "landlocked" by private property far below. During prehistoric times, the entire Horsethief Trail route was an important trans-mountain route from the coast to the inland valleys.

At 5.8 miles, amid a patch of Coulter pines and incense-cedars, you come to Los Pinos Saddle. At the northwest corner of a large, cleared area in the saddle itself, find the old roadbed (Trabuco Canyon Trail) angling downward along the shady slopes of Trabuco Canyon's main fork. Thick stands of live oak and big-cone Douglas fir keep this part of the trail dark and gloomy during the fall and winter months, and delightfully cool at other times. Flowering currant and ceanothus shrubs at the trailside brighten things up in the spring.

One mile below the saddle, the trail veers left, crosses a divide, and begins descending along a tributary of Trabuco Canyon. You walk by thickets of California bay (bay laurel), which exude an enigmatically pleasant/pungent scent. After crossing the tributary ravine twice, the trail clings to a dry and sunny south-facing slope. Down below, in an almost inaccessible section of the ravine, you may hear water trickling and tumbling over boulders half-hidden under tangles of underbrush and trees. Before long, you arrive back at the junction of the Horsethief Trail in shady Trabuco Canyon, and continue down to the trailhead.

Area M-2: Santa Ana Mountains— Ortega Corridor

From San Juan Capistrano to Lake Elsinore, Highway 74—Ortega Highway—stretches like a snake over the midsection of the Santa Ana Mountains. Leisurely rising from the west through San Juan Canyon to the oak-dotted crest, then descending the east escarpment via sharp curves, the road gives casual tourists their only glimpse of the interior Santa Anas.

The highway commemorates Jose Francisco Ortega, sergeant and scout in the Portola party, which in 1769 passed through Orange County's coastal hills while heading up the California coast. The present roadway, completed in 1933, followed a turn-of-the-century wagon track, which in turn evolved from the route of a centuries-old Juaneno Indian Trail. The highway's rustic character remains, much to the delight of the unhurried sightseer but not the growing numbers of frustrated commuters who race along it daily to and from employment

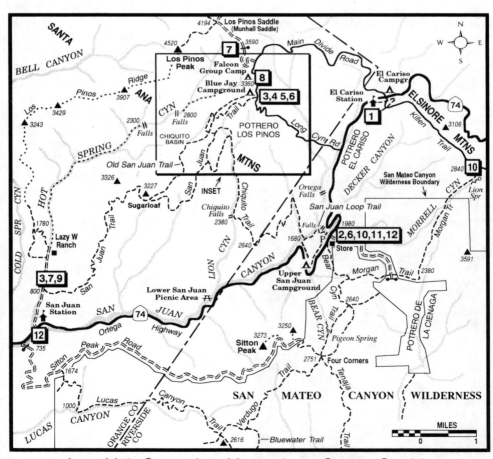

Area M-2: Santa Ana Mountains—Ortega Corridor

centers in southern Orange County.

The Forest Service recognizes Ortega Highway as an important recreational corridor. Campground facilities have been constructed and several trailheads have been developed. But few roads penetrate the backcountry areas, and foot trails are the usual way of getting around.

Day hiking (along with mountain biking and horseback riding) and car camping are popular in the Ortega Corridor. Overnight backpacking is allowed south of the highway, but only within San Mateo Canyon Wilderness (see Area M-3 for complete coverage of this area).

Developed camping facilities are found at Caspers Wilderness Park (Area F-5), and in several areas within the national forest. The national-forest facilities include the always-open El Cariso Camp-

ground and the seasonally open Upper San Juan Campground. Both lie along Ortega Highway and therefore can get considerable traffic noise. Delightful and secluded Blue Jay Campground rests high in the remote Potrero Los Pinos area, north of Ortega Highway. Blue Jay Campground and its neighbor, Falcon Group Camp (for large groups with reservations), are open seasonally, from May until November.

The drive up Ortega Highway is an enjoyable prelude to a day's hiking activities. Starting from the San Juan Capistrano side, the highway runs through outlying suburban development, rolling hills still used for grazing, and the rugged foothills of Caspers Wilderness Park. Past Caspers you come to San Juan Fire Station and the national-forest boundary. On ahead Ortega Highway winds along

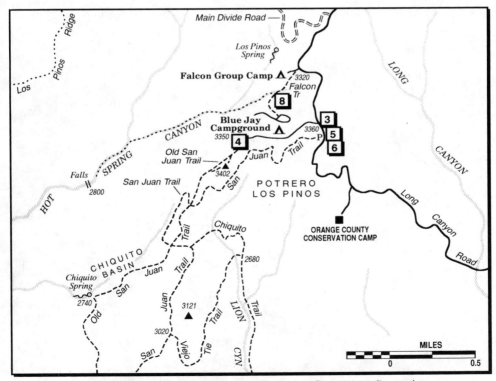

Santa Ana Mountains—Ortega Corridor (inset)

the precipitous south wall of San Juan Canyon, passing Lower San Juan Picnic Area and Upper San Juan Campground. A major trailhead is located next to the Ortega Oaks Store (also called the "candy store"), 0.7 mile past Upper San Juan Campground. From here, trails lead north into the Potrero Los Pinos area and south into San Mateo Canyon Wilderness. Up the road another 1.6 miles is a large turnout on the left (west) side of the road. From there you can drop down any of several short, steep paths into the can-

yon bottom to the west and visit Ortega Falls (not labeled on most maps). The falls are seasonal, showing a mere trickle of water most of the year; however, the sheer rock exposures here are popular year-round among rock climbers.

After another mile Ortega Highway levels out in a pleasant oak woodland (Potrero El Cariso). Long Canyon Road, intersecting on the left (west), climbs higher to another oak-dotted area—Potrero Los Pinos—and Blue Jay Campground. A little over a mile past

Lower falls in lower Hot Spring Canyon

Long Canyon Road, Ortega Highway passes the El Cariso Ranger Station and Visitor Information Center (open daily; maps and information available) and El Cariso Campground.

Just east of that, Main Divide Road (renamed the Killen Trail on the south side of the highway) crosses Ortega Highway, providing access to areas along the Main Divide of the Santa Ana Mountains to the north, and to the Elsinore Mountains to the south. A little farther on, Ortega Highway begins its abrupt descent to Lake Elsinore. Wending your way through the community of Lake Elsinore, you can pick up Interstate 15, which will take you back to Orange County if you use I-15 north and take the Riverside Freeway (Highway 91) west at Corona.

Trip 1: El Cariso Nature Trail

Distance	1.3 miles
Total Elevation Gain/Loss	150'/150'
Hiking Time	1 hour
Optional Map	USGS 7.5-min *Alberhill*
Best Times	All year
Agency	CNF/TD
Difficulty	★

If you're not very familiar with the natural history of the Santa Ana Mountains, stop first at El Cariso Station along Ortega Highway. Inside the small visitor center here you'll find some small but instructive exhibits on the local flora, fauna, and geology. To learn even more pick up the El Cariso Nature Trail self-guiding leaflet, then walk the trail itself, which begins just behind the visitor building.

The opportunity to become familiar with common varieties of native shrubs is the real value of taking this short walk. You'll see examples of chamise, buckwheat, manzanita, scrub oak, sugar bush, and three types of sage. In spring, monkeyflower, blue-eyed grass, nightshade, and other vivid-hued annual flowers compete for attention, while the blooms of wild peony nod circumspectly close to the ground. Amid the tangled branches of the shrubs look for the spiny, green fruits of the wild cucumber.

After a very brief passage under some oaks, the trail begins winding moderately upward on a chaparral- and sage-covered slope. The view to the west is of rolling country dotted with small houses on large lots (the area around El Cariso is a patchwork of national-forest and private lands).

Soon the trail levels out and turns east to circle a hilltop, passing an old mine shaft. Then it descends slightly to cross the Killen Trail (a paved road). Continue diagonally across the road and pick up the remainder of the trail, harder to follow now. After meandering through a grove of "Penny Pines"—mostly Coulter pines, but some oak, incense-cedar and cypress trees—you arrive back at the starting point.

Trip 2: San Juan Loop Trail

Distance	2.1 miles
Total Elevation Gain/Loss	350'/350'
Hiking Time	1 hour
Optional Map	USGS 7.5-min *Sitton Peak*
Best Times	October through June
Agency	CNF/TD
Difficulty	★

If you've no more time to spare than an hour while cruising the Ortega Highway, at least stop and try the San Juan Loop Trail (not to be confused with the much longer San Juan Trail, Trip 3). Sights include a small waterfall along San Juan Creek, excellent wildflower displays in the spring, and some of the finest oak woodland in the Santa Anas.

Park in the large lot directly across from the Ortega Oaks Store. From here pick up the well-worn path leading north, slightly uphill, along the slope overlooking the highway. After curving left and dropping a little, the trail threads the side

of a narrow gorge resounding—in the wet season at least—with falling water. A spur trail leads down toward the lip of the falls; from there you can hop over to a reflecting pool and maybe settle into the polished granite for a moment's quiet meditation. A single gnarled juniper clings sentinel-like to a bouldered slope overlooking the pool, far from its usual habitat on desert slopes 50 or more miles north and east.

From the falls area, you descend on easy switchbacks through the chaparral and reach, after more than ½ mile, an oak-dotted flat along San Juan Creek. Soon the Chiquito Trail branches north to cross the

Reflecting pool at top of falls on San Juan Loop Trail

creek. The loop trail bears left (south) to follow Bear Canyon beside Ortega Highway. For a delightful few minutes as you walk here, the sky's brilliance is muted by the arching limbs of centuries-old live oaks, and the soft ground on the trailside is aglow with the seasonal greens, browns, and reds of ferns, poison-oak leaves, and wild grasses.

Touching briefly the perimeter of Upper San Juan Campground, the trail veers sharply left to gain an open slope, again parallel to the highway. Continue for another 0.5 mile across this sun-struck slope, dotted with wildflowers in the spring, and arrive back at the parking lot.

Trip 3: San Juan Trail

Distance	11 miles
Total Elevation Gain/Loss	550'/3100'
Hiking Time	5 hours
Optional Maps	Cleveland National Forest recreation map; USGS 7.5-min *Alberhill, Sitton Peak, Canada Gobernadora*
Best Times	November through May
Agency	CNF/TD
Difficulty	★★★

With gentle grades most of the way, the San Juan Trail is tailor-made for a leisurely saunter from the Main Divide of the Santa Anas to the lower foothills. Since the trail runs largely along dry ridgelines exposed to the sun, hot days should be scrupulously avoided. Clear winter days bring out the best in the scenery: on some occasions the view takes in much of the southern Orange County coastline and Santa Catalina and San Clemente islands. Due to an elevation change of about 2500 feet, most of the spring wildflowers common to the chaparral and sage-scrub plant associations can be seen somewhere and sometime along this trail.

Transportation arrangements for this one-way trip are relatively uncomplicated. The lower trailhead lies in Hot Spring Canyon, 0.8 mile north of the San Juan Fire Station on Ortega Highway, and the upper trailhead lies just south of the entrance to Blue Jay Campground.

In this description I'll route you along the newer version of the San Juan Trail,

originally an Indian trail but now built to modern standards with switchbacks where needed. Shortcuts using older and more direct sections of the trail (shown on our Area M-2 inset map) may be taken if you want to save a little time. There are many trail junctions along the way, so pay attention to the following directions. The latest (photorevised 1982) editions of the topo maps listed above do not show the alignment of the new trail precisely. The October 1993 wildfire, one of many that devastated Southern California that month, burned across much of the San Juan Trail. Since then, the regrowth of sage-scrub and chaparral vegetation has been rapid.

Begin at the small roadside parking area 100 yards south of the entrance to Blue Jay Campground (the Forest Service is contemplating building another, larger trailhead parking area to replace this one). From here the "new" San Juan Trail winds west and south around the heads of two shady canyons, just below the level of the campground. After about one mile, the trail

Alder thicket, west end of San Juan Trail

San Juan Trail bends right to cross the top of a gentle divide, and the Viejo Tie Trail, on the left, goes along the hillside.

Stay on the San Juan Trail, which now bears south-southwest through more chaparral. Reaching some oaks in a ravine bottom (3.7 miles), the trail zigzags a couple of times through grass and poison oak and crosses an intermittent stream. Enjoy the shade: this is the last grove of trees until you come to the end of the trail in Hot Spring Canyon.

On the far side of the ravine, the trail swings south of a peaklet (2966'), and then climbs moderately toward a flat area (5.0 miles) just south of Sugarloaf, where the old trail, a rutted firebreak at this point, comes in from the right. A short but tough climb to Sugarloaf's summit can be made from here, over big granitic boulders and through brush.

After dropping down along the west slope of Sugarloaf, you come to a saddle overlooking Hot Spring Canyon to the north. The terrain in view suggests a possible direct route into this canyon, a way to reach the big waterfall at the 2300-foot level (see Trip 9), but hidden from your line of sight are several hundred vertical feet of steep, brushy terrain calling for some serious bushwhacking. Looking toward the distant north, you'll spot the flat-topped, antenna-crowded summit of Santiago Peak.

The gradual descent continues, largely on or near the spine of a ridge offering nice views of other ridges and canyons in every direction. Far below to the south, the gray blacktop of Ortega Highway resembles a giant snake propelling it-

starts descending along a sunny, sage-carpeted slope. At 1.3 miles the new trail, the one you're on, crosses the old trail, a steep, rocky roadbed, and plunges into the deep shade of a ravine. For a time, live oaks keep the sun's rays at bay.

After rounding a single switchback and descending further, you reach, in a sunny, sage-dotted clearing at 1.7 miles, a second crossing of the old trail, which from here leads to Chiquito Basin and then back up to join the new trail again just below Sugarloaf peak. Keep straight and come to a junction, 1.8 miles, with the Chiquito Trail. Stay right here.

Continue south along the base of a hillside, through some tall and dense chaparral. Climbing slightly into a more sparsely vegetated zone, you arrive, 2.4 miles (3020'), at another junction, where the self through the sycamores in San Juan Canyon.

The granite boulders and decomposed granite soil seen earlier along the trail are not here; the trail now is hewn into friable metasedimentary rock, the same kind of metamorphosed sea-floor sediment typically found in Silverado and Trabuco canyons to the north.

At around 8.5 miles, several switchbacks take you safely down a crumbling slope. East of these switchbacks, a sharply folded anticline can be seen in the rock strata. To the west, other switchbacks on an earlier version of the trail can be spotted. At 10.0 miles, with only a mile to go, you begin descending quickly. A final set of zigzags takes you down into Hot Spring Canyon, where the trail intersects the road coming up from San Juan Fire Station.

Trip 4: Chiquito Basin

Distance	2.8 miles
Total Elevation Gain/Loss	700'/700'
Hiking Time	2 hours (round trip)
Optional Map	USGS 7.5-min *Alberhill*
Best Times	All year
Agency	CNF/TD
Difficulty	★★

A Forest Service brochure describes this as a nice morning hike for those camping at Blue Jay Campground or Falcon Group Camp. The earlier the better, I might add. I discovered fresh tracks of a deer and a mountain lion both apparently moving along at a running gait one wet morning in the soft surface of the trail. With an earlier start I might have witnessed a terrific chase.

In this description you start from the west edge of Blue Jay Campground, 0.4 mile west of the entrance, and then take the most direct route to Chiquito Basin—the old San Juan Trail. If the campground is closed, park outside the gate and pick up the new San Juan Trail skirting the campground (see Trip 3), or simply walk through the campground itself to reach the beginning of the old trail at the campground's west end.

The wide, rocky path of the old San Juan Trail leads southwest along the ridgeline past some walk-in campsites shaded by oaks and tall chaparral, and then pitches downhill. At 0.6 mile and again at 0.8 mile the new San Juan Trail, with its gentler but longer grade, crosses the old one. Keep straight to save time. Between these two crossings, white sage uniformly carpets the slopes on both sides of the old trail; in springtime its dull, grayish foliage is upstaged by Indian paintbrush, a plant thought to be parasitic on the roots of sage.

Continue downhill into the oak-rimmed meadow informally called Chiquito Basin. This is a great place for birdwatching, picnicking, or loafing. From the western corner of the meadow a faint trail leads to Chiquito Spring, named by early Cleveland Forest ranger Kenneth Munhall, who stopped there one warm afternoon in 1927 with his horse, Chiquito. The spring is bedecked with giant chain ferns and poison-oak vines, and buzzes with insects. On the poison-oak-infested slope north of the spring, you can find at least half a dozen *morteros*—Indian grinding holes worn into the granitic bedrock.

Return the same way, or if the spirit moves you, explore further. From the edge of Chiquito Basin, the old San Juan Trail veers south and climbs 300 vertical feet up a steep, oak-shaded slope to reach an open ridgetop offering a fine view of the basin and its surroundings. The old trail then turns southwest along this ridgeline and connects with the new San Juan Trail at the base of Sugarloaf peak. From here you might loop back to Blue Jay Campground by following the twists and turns of the new trail, if you have time.

Trip 5: Viejo Tie Loop

Distance	5.5 miles
Total Elevation Gain/Loss	1000'/1000'
Hiking Time	3 hours
Optional Map	USGS 7.5-min *Alberhill*
Best Times	November through June
Agency	CNF/TD
Difficulty	★★

In Orange County the most dependable and most lavish displays of springtime flowering take place in the chaparral plant community. Beginning with the longer days and warmer soil temperatures of March, and ending with the onset of heat and drought in May or June, the higher mountains are alive with the color and fragrance of blooming plants large and small.

This hike takes you into stands of mature chaparral, dotted here and there with live oak trees. Aside from the common white-blooming ceanothus, you may discover at the trailside more than a dozen kinds of wildflowers. Typical finds are red monkeyflower, nightshade, prickly phlox, aster, golden yarrow, cow parsnip, wild pea, wild hyacinth, Indian pink, and Mariposa lily.

Begin as in Trip 3 above, taking the new San Juan Trail for 2.4 miles. Then bear left on the Viejo Tie Trail. After swinging left around the brow of a ridge, you descend northward through tall chaparral to reach the oak-shaded bed of Lion Canyon. On the far bank, after a couple of switchbacks, you come to the Chiquito Trail. Turn left, climb 300 vertical feet back to the San Juan Trail, crossing the creek bed again, and return the way you came.

Trip 6: Chiquito Trail

Distance	9.2 miles
Total Elevation Gain/Loss	900'/2300'
Hiking Time	5 hours
Optional Maps	USGS 7.5-min *Alberhill, Sitton Peak*
Best Times	November through May
Agency	CNF/TD
Difficulty	★★★

Like the San Juan Trail, the Chiquito Trail is best explored from end to end, downhill direction preferred. Along the way you'll enjoy cool passages through canyon bottoms, but also endure (if the weather is warm) a seemingly endless traverse across a sun-blasted ridge.

Completed in 1974, the Chiquito Trail is easy to follow, yet it's potentially an ankle-twister. In places sharp rocks have eroded out of the decomposed granite bed of the trail, so it's necessary to watch your step.

Begin at the upper terminus of the San Juan Trail (see Trip 3) and descend, using the easy switchbacks, to the Chiquito Trail junction, 1.8 miles. Turn left (east) and descend into Lion Canyon, 0.2 mile away. The canyon has water about half the year.

The next couple of miles down-canyon are delightful, with patchy shade provided by large oaks—the survivors of wildfires—and young sycamores. On the banks of the creek you'll find poison oak, wild blackberry, toyon, barberry, and ceanothus. Profuse displays of monkeyflower brighten the scene in April. The red monkeyflower and the sticky (yellow-flowered) monkeyflower may have hybridized here: the spectrum of monkeyflower colors includes orange, pink, and magenta, as well as the usual scarlet and light-yellow hues.

At 4.2 miles the trail makes an abrupt bend to the left and begins a long traverse across the ridge to the east. Just below this bend is Chiquito Falls, where the stream drops about 15 feet over an outcrop of granite. Impressive only after heavy rains, the site is a pleasant one anytime for a picnic.

Rising through scrubby chaparral and granitic boulders, the trail works around to a south-facing slope. The din of traffic from Ortega Highway less than one bee-line mile away is enough to convince you the end is near, but it's not. Instead, the trail curves northeast and crookedly descends for another 2 miles to an unnamed tributary of San Juan Canyon. To occupy yourself on the way down, look for hawks and golden eagles riding the thermals, and squirrels or lizards scurrying around at ground level.

Upon reaching the bottom of the unnamed canyon, the trail turns south to follow an intermittent watercourse, similar to the creek in Lion Canyon. After another mile, you come to San Juan Canyon and the San Juan Loop Trail. Go either right or left around the loop to reach the large trailhead parking lot opposite the Ortega Oaks Store.

Trip 7: Los Pinos Ridge

Distance	10 miles
Total Elevation Gain/Loss	2400'/5200'
Hiking Time	7 hours
Recommended Maps	USGS 7.5-min *Alberhill, Santiago Peak, Canada Gobernadora*
Best Times	November through April
Agency	CNF/TD
Difficulty	★★★★

Although plotted as a trail on Forest Service and topographic maps, the Los Pinos ridge route has for many years received only irregular or no maintenance. Once a wide firebreak, it now serves as a throughway only for wildlife and a few adventurous humans. Clinging religiously to the undulating ridgeline, the route is tiring in its many uphills as well as its absurdly steep downhills. Prospective hikers should be ready to do battle with brush, and be equipped with tough trousers and sturdy shoes. Rattlesnakes may be a problem in warm weather; proceed slowly and cautiously through areas where you can't see the ground.

The greatest reward during the hike is the fine views west and south to the Pacific Ocean and the islands, east past Lake Elsinore to the highest summits of the Peninsular Ranges, and down into the V-

Bedrock **morteros,** *Chiquito Basin*

shaped upper gorges of Hot Spring and Bell canyons.

The Los Pinos Trail is designated by the Forest Service as "landlocked," which means that there is no public access at its lower end. If you plan to hike this route all the way through, as I describe here, you'll need permission to pass through the Lazy W Ranch church camp (P.O. Box 579, San Juan Capistrano 92675; phone 949-728-0141) at the lower end of the trail. Parking is not allowed at the church camp and is very limited near the camp's entrance, so if you're going to leave a car at the end of the hike, park it at the west end of the San Juan Trail, 0.8 mile north of Ortega Highway.

If you set up a car shuttle, leave one car at the lower (west) terminus of the San Juan Trail, 0.8 mile north of Ortega Highway in Hot Spring Canyon. Take the other car up Long Canyon Road past Blue Jay and Falcon campgrounds to Main Divide Road, then uphill another 0.6 mile to the big steel gate which is locked during motor-vehicle closures. This is your starting point. (A 4-wheel-drive vehicle could take you to Los Pinos Saddle, a.k.a. Munhall Saddle, when the road is open, May through October.)

From the gate, trudge up the steep road 1.2 miles to Los Pinos Saddle, where the Trabuco Canyon Trail joins Main Divide Road. Follow the wide firebreak going very steeply up the ridge to the southwest. The crumbly metasedimentary rock on the slope is a foretaste of what you will have to contend with in the miles ahead. Chamise, bush poppy, ceanothus, manzanita, and scattered Coulter pines keep a low profile along the ridge, allowing clear vistas in nearly every direction.

A mile from the saddle, you pass some fantastically weathered outcrops—part of a small exposure of the Santiago Peak Volcanics formation in this area. Nearby are surveyor's bench marks identifying Los Pinos Peak, fourth-highest named peak in the Santa Ana Mountains. (The three highest peaks—Santiago, Modjeska, and Trabuco—are on the Main Divide.) The true summit of the peak (elevation 4520+ feet) lies a little to the northeast of the bench marks.

Beyond Los Pinos Peak, the trail deteriorates. Over the next 3 miles, make sure you stay on the well-defined ridge between Hot Spring and Bell canyons. Scattered big-cone Douglas-firs struggle up the north-facing slopes, where the sun's drying effects are allayed. Coastal fog or haze sometimes fills the canyon bottoms. With the relief between ridgetop and canyon bottoms a somewhat sheer 1500 feet, you seem perched between two yawning abysses.

More and more chaparral and weedy plants choke the trail as you descend. As you grope through the brush just past peak 3429, be very careful to stay on the correct ridgeline: here the route turns south to follow the ridge between Cold Spring Canyon and a tributary of Hot Spring Canyon.

As you descend into a secluded little bowl drained by Cold Spring Canyon, the trail condition may improve. This section has in the past been cleared and maintained by members of the church camp. Eventually, you'll come to a trail junction. Go either way: straight ahead takes you along the ridgeline and then straight down to the lower end of the church property; left takes you down multiple switchbacks to the upper end of the camp. Wend your way through the camp, past the entrance, and then down the road to the parking lot at the west terminus of the San Juan Trail.

Trip 8: Upper Hot Spring Canyon

Distance	3.0 miles
Total Elevation Gain/Loss	450'/450'
Hiking Time	2½ hours (round trip)
Recommended Map	USGS 7.5-min *Alberhill*
Best Times	December through May
Agency	CNF/TD
Difficulty	★★★

Falls in upper Hot Spring Canyon

Silent, except for the gentle gurgle of water over stone, upper Hot Spring Canyon is an easy-to-reach retreat not far from the popular campgrounds in the Potrero Los Pinos area. Boulder-hopping and mild bushwhacking take you to an interesting area of small waterfalls and dark, limpid pools.

Start at either campground—Blue Jay or Falcon—and walk about halfway out the Falcon Trail, which connects the two. From there, drop down into a shallow gully to the west, using any one of several informal paths. Follow this gully downstream, dodging brush along the way. You'll soon join a bigger gully at the head of Hot Spring Canyon carrying water from Los Pinos Spring, which lies a short distance upstream. Memorize or mark this junction for the trip back.

A narrow, lightly beaten path goes down-canyon along grassy benches and across crumbly metasedimentary rock, crossing the creek several times. The canyon ahead trends consistently southwest, despite a few bends. You're following the Los Pinos Fault, an inactive fault running perpendicular to the Elsinore Fault and other faults responsible for the recent (in a geological sense) uplift of the Santa Ana Mountains.

Just before you reach the junction of a major, wet canyon to the north (2950 feet), there's a small waterfall and a grotto with two shallow pools. On the rocks, ferns, mosses, and a type of succulent "live-for-ever" descriptively known as "lady fingers" add to the charm. A cluster of alders grows nearby; they are found in increasing numbers downstream, all the way to San Juan Canyon.

After another 0.4 mile, the canyon bot-tom makes a bend to the right and drops abruptly. All but experienced climbers should stop here and go no farther. Intrepid climbers may want to try (very cautiously) working their way over the loose metamor-phic rock ahead to get a glimpse of a hidden 25-foot waterfall and a deep pool. Below this, the water shoots down a slot through pol-ished granite. (Note: The rock in this area is very loose and unstable. Standard rock-climbing techniques are of little value.)

Further progress down-canyon to-ward the big falls (read on—Trip 9) is pos-sible only by long and difficult traverses over the canyon walls to either side.

Trip 9: Lower Hot Spring Canyon

Distance	9.0 miles (to falls and back)
Total Elevation Gain/Loss	1600'/1600'
Hiking Time	10 hours (round trip)
Recommended Maps	USGS 7.5-min *Canada Gobernadora*, *Santiago Peak, Alberhill*
Best Times	December through March
Agency	CNF/TD
Difficulty	★★★★

This is a trip of superlatives—surely the most beautiful canyon hike in the Santa Ana Mountains. The goal is a magnificent 140-foot waterfall, one of southern California's highest. This is also a decep-tively difficult hike—in fact, it's the most strenuous, and objectively the most haz-ardous, of all the trips in this book.

Being in excellent physical condition, having considerable experience in cross-country travel over rugged terrain, and possessing good judgment do not auto-matically guarantee that you'll be able to reach the falls and return without mishap. You must be cautious, patient, and deter-mined too. Hazards include slippery rocks (some concealed by leaf litter), prickly veg-etation, and forests of poison oak. Long pants, a long-sleeved shirt, and sturdy

boots are musts.

Several factors determine the appro-priate time of year to take this trip. Autumn leaves put on a great show during Novem-ber and December, but if the rains are late, there won't be much water cascading over the falls or flowing down the creek. Wild-flowers and new leaves in early spring add to the canyon's beauty, but by then the ubiquitous poison oak bushes and vines are sporting fresh, virulent leaves, and rattlesnakes are emerging from their win-ter burrows. Most years, fair-weather days in January and February are best as long as you start early enough in the morning to take advantage of the limited daylight.

A portion of this route unavoidably passes through an inholding in the Na-tional Forest—the Lazy W Ranch, a church camp. You must ask for permission to hike through the property in advance. Write Lazy W Ranch, P.O. Box 579, San Juan Capistrano, CA 92675 (include SASE), or phone the caretaker at (949) 728-0141 to obtain permission. The caretaker may ask that you inform someone of your safe return on your way out.

Parking is not allowed at the church camp and is very limited near the camp's entrance, so leave your car at the lower (west) San Juan Trail terminus, 0.8 mile north of Ortega Highway. Walk 0.6 mile north to the church camp entrance, then continue another 0.3 mile past several buildings, staying close to the creek all the while. Walk around a chain-link vehicle gate, and continue up an old roadbed flanked on both sides by huge, spreading coast live oak trees.

By 1.5 miles (from your car), the route deteriorates to little more than a game trail. The creek bubbles alongside, with scattered sycamores and alders growing from the granite-bouldered banks. At 2.0 miles, the canyon makes a decided turn to the northeast. From this point on, dark brownish and grayish metamorphic rocks gradually replace the granites, and the canyon becomes considerably narrower. Progress is slowed by a factor of two or three. You must choose between battling thickets of willow, sage, wild blackberry, and poison oak on the banks, or rock-hopping and sloshing through the creek while dodging nettles and alder branches. Here and there the creek may disappear under porous sands for brief stretches.

At 3.4 miles (1620 feet),

the creek slides over a series of granite slabs and collects in limpid pools almost perennially shaded by an overhanging south wall. Fallen sycamore, oak, and alder leaves dimple the water's mirror-like surface. On the north bank, a smooth granite slab, perfect for lounging, catches early-afternoon winter sunlight; it's a nice place to rest on your return down-canyon if you have time. Just beyond, the canyon broadens, and a usually wet tributary, draining Chiquito Basin, comes in on the right. At

Lower falls in Hot Spring canyon

In lower Hot Spring canyon

4.1 miles (1950 feet), another usually wet tributary joins on the left; a 70-foot waterfall with a scant flow lies immediately up this triburary from the main canyon.

By now, it should be possible to glimpse, just 200 yards ahead, the top of a sheer headwall. From the lip, water plunges an estimated 140 feet down two distinct tiers. Some boulder-hopping will get you to the base of a much smaller fall (a moss-covered 20-footer) just below the bottom of the big one, but further progress directly up canyon is possible only by some dicey hand-and-toe climbing.

To reach the base of the main falls, you can try backtracking a little and scrambling up the steep, broken slope to the south. As you do so, look for a well-used raptor's aerie on a banded cliff wall to the north.

The top of the main falls can be reached by making long traverses either right or left; from there it's possible, with great effort, to continue up canyon toward the upper series of falls described in Trip 8.

Trip 10: Morgan Trail

Distance	5.0 miles
Total Elevation Gain/Loss	350'/1200'
Hiking Time	2½ hours
Recommended Maps	USGS 7.5-min *Alberhill, Sitton Peak*
Best Times	October through May
Agency	CNF/TD
Difficulty	★★

As I rambled down the Morgan Trail one crisp autumn morning before dawn, the crackling of oak leaves underfoot played counterpoint to the drone of a hundred crickets singing in unison. Dozens of cold, blue stars sparkled overhead; while the moon's beams, caught in a tangled aerial net of limbs and branches, painted the ground in shades of black, gray, and silvery white. These simple kinds of sensations, jelled together, added up to a pow-

erful, almost mystical, experience.

The Morgan Trail crosses the northern edge of San Mateo Canyon Wilderness, one of coastal southern California's newest national-forest wilderness areas and possibly its last. You can camp overnight along portions of the trail within the wilderness boundary, but don't forget the required wilderness camping permit (see the introduction to Area M-3 for details). This description assumes you are going to hike the trail one-way—in the north-to-south, predominantly downhill direction.

To reach the starting point, leave Highway 74 at a point 0.3 mile east of El Cariso Station and drive 2.7 miles up the Killen Trail (formerly South Main Divide Road) to a signed trailhead parking area on the right (west) side. As you drive up you can enjoy spectacular vistas of Lake Elsinore to the east, with its backdrop bald hills and distant mountains. On weekends this stretch of road is a favorite launching area for hang-gliders.

On the trail you quickly drop through manzanita and other chaparral and join the promenade of live oaks in Morrell Canyon. Willows and a few sycamores hug the canyon bottom, where water flows during the wet season. Going just this far (5 or 10 minutes in) is rewarding in itself if you have little time. At 1.0 mile the trail cuts left (south) across the creek and rises to higher and sunnier terrain. Soon you're back on chaparral-covered slopes, dotted with granitic boulders.

At around 2.3 miles, the trail (following an old dirt road at this point) goes west along the perimeter of private lands in

Oak woodland along Morgan Trail

Potrero de la Cienaga and Round Potrero. At 2.7 miles, the narrow tread resumes and the trail continues west in thick chaparral. At 3.5 miles you begin a crooked descent into some oak woods, where you join the Bear Canyon Trail (4.0 miles). Stay right and continue another mile downhill to the Bear Canyon trailhead adjacent to the Ortega Oaks Store.

Trip 11: Sitton Peak

Distance	9.5 miles
Total Elevation Gain/Loss	2150'/2150'
Hiking Time	5 hours (round trip)
Recommended Map	USGS 7.5-min *Sitton Peak*
Best Times	October through May
Agency	CNF/TD
Difficulty	★★★

From below, Sitton Peak looks unimposing—a mere bump on a rambling ridge—despite its distinction as one of the highest points in the Santa Ana Mountains south of Ortega Highway. On the summit, though, the feeling is decidedly "top of the world." When an east or north wind blows,

cleansing the sky of water vapor and air pollution, 50-mile vistas in every direction are not uncommon.

The hike to the summit is always a peaceful one, because it passes through lands included in San Mateo Canyon Wilderness. Trail camping is allowed within the wilderness area, provided you obtain the necessary free permit from the Forest Service (see introduction to Area M-3).

Begin by taking the Bear Canyon Trail south from the Ortega Oaks Store. Before long you pass into San Mateo Canyon Wilderness, where mountain bikes are banned (though wheel tracks are sometimes in evidence). After 1.0 mile of moderate ascent, you come to a trail junction in the midst of a small oak woodland. Go right (as the Morgan Trail forks left) and begin climbing more steeply along a chaparral-clothed slope. At about 1.9 miles, you reach a summit and then you descend slightly to the old Verdugo Truck Trail, now part of the Bear Canyon Trail. You can either turn right, on an old truck trail, or continue straight across on a newer and narrower trail (an alternate, slightly longer route). Both lead to Four Corners—originally a 4-way meeting of roads, and a 5-way trail junction now.

The old route to Four Corners, going south down a brushy draw flanked by blue-flowering ceanothus, is a bit more scenic. At 2.7 miles on the old route you arrive at oak-shaded Pigeon Spring, a seasonal (nonpotable) source at the head of Bear Canyon. An old watering trough is here, with seeps nearby. Enjoy the shade—you won't find much more of it ahead.

Continue south another 0.5 mile to Four Corners, and swing right on the wide path climbing northwest—a disused section of the Sitton Peak Road. After a steady ascent of about 300 vertical feet, you reach a flat area (4.0 miles) just below a boulder-studded ridge, with a 3250-foot high point, to the north. Easily climbed, the ridge summit offers a view somewhat similar to that seen from Sitton Peak. The flat area by the road (just inside the wilderness boundary) makes a good overnight campsite for those who backpack in.

Beyond the flat area the road descends another 0.5 mile to a saddle just below Sitton Peak. From this saddle, you leave the road and follow a steep, informal trail up through scattered manzanita and chamise on the east slope of the peak.

The view from the top is especially impressive to the west. Here the foothills and western canyons of the Santa Anas merge with the creeping suburbs of southern Orange County. Beyond lies the flat, blue ocean punctuated by the profile of Santa Catalina Island. Some 2000 feet below, toylike cars on the highway make their way down the sinuous course of San Juan Canyon.

Trip 12: Lucas Canyon

Distance	14 miles
Total Elevation Gain/Loss	2000'/3200'
Hiking Time	7 hours
Recommended Maps	USGS 7.5-min *Sitton Peak, Canada Gobernadora*; Cleveland National Forest San Mateo Canyon Wilderness map
Best Times	November through May
Agency	CNF/TD
Difficulty	★★★★

Under construction for years, primarily through the efforts of volunteer workers, the Lucas Canyon Trail was finally completed in 1992. The opening of the trail inaugurated the first legal access to the San Mateo Canyon Wilderness trail system from the west. Shortly thereafter, in October 1993, virtually all of the vegetation traversed by the trail was incinerated to ash and blackened twigs when flames swept through. Late in 1993, before the first substantial rains had fallen, I hiked the trail and discovered a landscape far more moonlike in appearance than anything I'd seen before. Some hillsides were reduced to nothing but rock and soil. Flat, gray patches of ash marked where car-sized shrubs once stood.

Only 18 months later, the whole area had experienced a riot of growth. The Lucas Canyon Trail, washed out in many sections and in danger of being completely smothered by pioneering vegetation, needed attention again. As of this writing, volunteers have pitched in to reconstruct and brush out the most troublesome sections. Some sections remain rough and possibly overgrown, so be sure to check with the Forest Service first if you are planning a trip on this trail.

Lucas Canyon has been called Orange County's "Mother Lode"—an overstated reference to the placer mining activity that took place here in the late 1800s. If you see old mining debris in the canyon, remember that it is considered "historical" and therefore must be left as is.

To make things interesting, plan a car shuttle and try exploring Lucas Canyon as part of a point-to-point trip, as described here. The trip begins at the Ortega Oaks Store ("Candy Store") along Ortega Highway, and ends at San Juan Fire Station. Plenty of parking space is available at both ends. Nearly 90 percent of the route lies within the boundary of San Mateo Canyon Wilderness, where you may camp overnight (by Forest Service permit only—see introduction to Area M-3). The last segment unavoidably passes through Caspers Wilderness Park; for that stretch you must obtain a hiker's permit at the Caspers Park entrance.

Begin, as in Trip 11 above, by following the Bear Canyon Trail south to the Four Corners trail junction, 3.2 miles. From there, take the Verdugo Trail (old Verdugo Truck Trail) southwest across dry, chaparral-coated hillsides. At 5.8 miles, the Bluewater Trail intersects on the left. Keep straight and bend right (west) through a shady oak woodland to the next trail junction (6.3 miles), just north of a rounded 2616-foot hill. Here, at the edge of the 1993 burn, turn right and head north on the Lucas Canyon Trail.

Nearly 3 miles of sometimes-steep descent lie ahead. To the south, you may spot some houses on the nearby ridgeline; these are part of the Rancho Carrillo development—an inholding in the wilderness area. After a long mile, these signs of civilization disappear as you descend on switchbacks over rough, rocky terrain. The bottom of Lucas Canyon, a steep gorge at this point, lies to your left. You cross the stream in the bottom of this gorge at 8.5 miles, traverse for a while along the south wall of the gorge, and descend again to the stream, which in this area flows about half the year. For the next 1.5 miles, the trail sticks close to the stream, and you may see evidence hereabouts of past gold-mining.

At 10.0 miles, the trail leaves the stream, bending northward along a small tributary toward the ridge above. At 11.5 miles you strike that ridge and turn right on an old truck trail. This brings you to Sitton Peak Road in less than half a mile. Turn left there and make a winding, nearly 2-mile descent to Ortega Highway. Turn right and walk ¼ mile along the highway to San Juan Fire Station, the nearest available parking spot.

Area M-3: Santa Ana Mountains—
San Mateo Canyon Wilderness

Down along the creek, a warm breeze carries the scent of sage and blooming chaparral. There's no sound but the distant drone of bees, the soft music of water coursing down polished rock, and your own footsteps. A fat gopher snake lounging by the creek stiffens at your approach. Tiny fish dart about in the stream eddies, while a pond turtle launches itself from a rock shelf, deftly slicing through the surface of a crystalline pool. You might as well be a thousand miles away from civilization.

This is the world of San Mateo Canyon, the heart of one of California's newest wilderness areas, the 62-square-mile San Mateo Canyon Wilderness. Carved out of the southernmost one-third of the Cleveland National Forest's Trabuco District, this charming but rugged area lies within 30 airline miles of 5 million people. Only 10 miles away are the expanding edges of three of the nation's fastest-growing suburban regions: southern Orange County, southwestern Riverside County, and northern San Diego County.

San Mateo Canyon may seem a short distance away by the map, but getting there may prove problematical. Some access roads receive little maintenance and may become impassable in wet weather. Exploring the inner sanctum of the wilderness can be both physically taxing and mentally stimulating; trails may melt into the scenery, and you can lose track of your position. But these difficulties are exactly what shields the area from casual users. If you're willing to put up with them, this is your paradise.

Prepare to make a long day of it, or pack in enough equipment to stay a night or two along the trail. Unlike many national-forest wilderness areas in California, which require wilderness permits for both day and overnight use, this one requires a permit only for overnight use (backpacking). Camping regulations emphasize the importance of fire control. Campfires are never allowed within the wilderness, though backpacking stoves are permitted if used within areas cleared of flammable vegetation. No mountain bikes are allowed either, in accordance with a general prohibition of mechanical conveyances—even wheeled carts—in all federal wilderness areas.

Wilderness camping permits can be obtained at the El Cariso Visitor Information Center at El Cariso Station on Ortega Highway, and at any Cleveland National Forest fire or ranger station. Since many of the ranger and fire stations keep irregular hours during the rainy months, it may be best to apply well in advance by mail or phone to the Trabuco Ranger District office in Corona (see Appendix 5). The Corona office is also your best source for information about national-forest road conditions.

Three primary entrance points have been designated for San Mateo Canyon Wilderness. The northern two are the San Juan Loop trailhead, across from the Ortega Oaks Store on Ortega Highway, and the Morgan trailhead on Killen Trail—the road formerly known as South Main Divide Road. This book's Area M-2 map shows these entrances best.

The primary entrance to the south half of the wilderness is from the new Tenaja trailhead, next to Tenaja Station. From most parts of Orange County, it takes 80 or 90 minutes to get there. To reach the Tenaja trailhead, drive south on Interstate

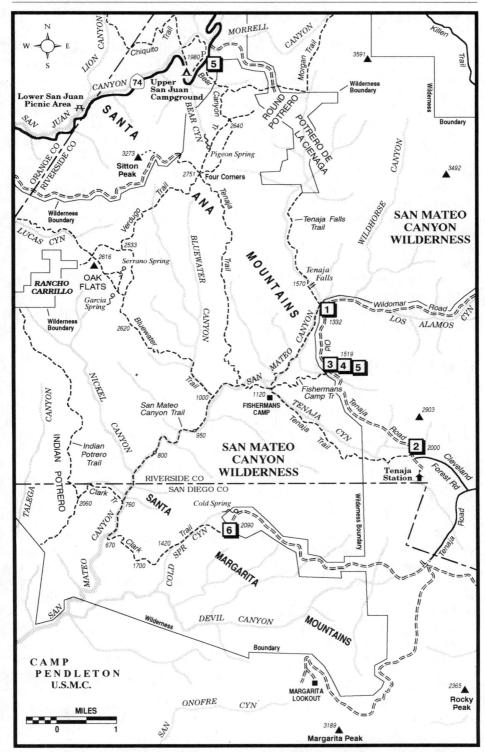

Area M-3: Santa Ana Mountains—San Mateo Canyon Wilderness

15 from Corona and exit at Clinton Keith Road in the community of Murrieta. Proceed 5 miles south on Clinton Keith Road and then 1.7 miles west on Tenaja Road to a marked intersection, where you must turn right to stay on Tenaja Road. Continue west on Tenaja Road for another 4.2 miles, then go right on one-lane, paved Cleveland Forest Road. Proceed another mile to the trailhead parking area, just north of Tenaja Station.

From the end of Tenaja Road it's possible to explore (using a 4-wheel-drive vehicle or truck, or a mountain bike) primitive roads along the east and south edge of the wilderness. Heading south you can reach the abandoned Margarita fire lookout atop the highest ridge in the Santa Margarita Mountains. From there the view encompasses Camp Pendleton, the coast, and the foreboding trench of Devil Canyon to the north.

Heading north from the Tenaja Trailhead, you can follow the unpaved "old" Tenaja Road down to secondary trailheads (turnouts in the road) at Fishermans Camp Trail (for Trips 3, 4, 5 in this section) and for accessing the lower end of the Tenaja Falls Trail. If you continue east and north on Wildomar Road and Killen Trail, you eventually reach Ortega Highway. This beautiful route follows cottonwood-choked Los Alamos Canyon, then runs along the crest of the Elsinore Mountains, offering spectacular views of Lake Elsinore and the distant mountains east and north. However, this route back to Orange County is usually *not* a time-saver, and you should never attempt it in an ordinary car. Several miles of Wildomar Road are a challenge even for high-clearance 4-wheel drives.

Trip 1: Tenaja Falls

Distance	1.4 miles
Total Elevation Gain/Loss	300'/300'
Hiking Time	1 hour (round trip)
Optional Map	USGS 7.5-min *Sitton Peak*
Best Times	December through June
Agency	CNF/TD
Difficulty	★

With five tiers and a total drop of about 150 feet, Tenaja Falls is the most interesting natural feature in San Mateo Canyon Wilderness. In late winter and spring, water coursing down the polished rock produces a kind of soothing music not widely heard in this somewhat dry corner of the Santa Ana Mountains.

A new trail, planned for the late 1990s, will skirt the private lands of Potrero de la Cienaga and provide fairly direct hiking access to Tenaja Falls via the Morgan Trail and Tenaja Falls Trail—a one-way trek of about 6 miles. Meanwhile, the only easy way to reach the falls is to endure (or enjoy, depending on your inclination) a long, bone-shaking drive from Ortega Highway in the north, or from Tenaja Road in the south. From the Ortega Highway side, follow the paved Killen Trail south to Wildomar Campground and ORV area. Beyond, the severely rutted Wildomar Road (Forest Road 7S04), for high-clearance 4-wheel-drive vehicles only, continues to a large turnout on the right (16 miles from Ortega Highway) overlooking the tree-covered bottom of San Mateo Canyon. This is the current Tenaja Falls trailhead. The Tenaja Road approach from the south is longer, but easier on your vehicle: From the Tenaja trailhead at the end of Rancho California Road, drive north 4.3 miles north on the unpaved "old" Tenaja Road to reach the same trailhead.

On foot, head down to the creek and cross it on the concrete ford of an old roadbed. If you can't balance on the row of rocks set there, then resign yourself to wading through. Continue north on the steadily rising roadbed and you'll soon be treated to a fairly distant view of the falls. After 0.7 mile the road passes near the up-

per lip of the falls, where a few large oaks provide welcome shade.

Further exploration of the falls requires real rock-climbing skills and extreme caution. The flow of water has worn the granitic rock almost glassy smooth. While scouting the middle tiers and pools, I found that slightly wet bare feet provided much more traction than the soles of my running shoes. Don't be lured into dangerous situations though.

A somewhat safer way of approaching the lower falls is to scramble over the rough-textured rocks well away from the water. You could also backtrack down the road and then scramble down the slope into the brush-choked creekbed down near the base of the falls.

Upper tier, Tenaja Falls

Trip 2: Tenaja Canyon

Distance	7.4 miles (to Fishermans Camp and back)
Total Elevation Gain/Loss	1300'/1300'
Hiking Time	3½ hours (round trip)
Optional Maps	USGS 7.5-min *Wildomar, Sitton Peak*
Best Times	November through May
Agency	CNF/TD
Difficulty	★★★

As the gloom of a late afternoon descends upon the deep-cut, linear furrow of Tenaja Canyon, dozens of orange-bellied newts waddle determinedly uphill and across the trail, oblivious to my footfalls. The cute faces and beady eyes of these little amphibians reflect a mindless desire I cannot fathom: Sex in a bower of leaf litter and ferns? A bellyful of succulent insects, ripe for the taking?

With the recent completion of the Tenaja Trail in the Santa Ana Mountains, the newts of Tenaja Canyon have been getting cross traffic of the hiker and horse types. The trail, and a fancy new trailhead built to serve it, has opened parts of San Mateo Canyon Wilderness area to ready access; no longer is it necessary to rattle down horrendous dirt roads to reach any sort of decent trail.

It is best to approach the Tenaja Trailhead from the south. Exit Interstate 15 at Clinton Keith Road, proceed 5 miles south on Clinton Keith Road and 1.7 miles west on Tenaja Road to a marked intersection, where you must turn right to stay on Tenaja Road. Continue west on Tenaja Road for another 4.2 miles, then go right on one-lane, paved Cleveland Forest Road. Proceed another mile to the trailhead parking area, just north of Tenaja Station.

An old-fashioned hand pump dispenses cold, sweet water at the trailhead.

Oak woodland at Fisherman's Camp

Sign in at the self-registration box, and head downhill on the trail going west. A few minutes' descent takes you to the shady bowels of **V**-shaped Tenaja Canyon, where huge coast live oaks and pale-barked sycamores frame a limpid, rock-dimpled stream. Mostly the trail ahead meanders alongside the stream, but for the canyon's middle stretch it carves its way across the chaparral-blanketed south wall, 200–400 feet above the canyon bottom.

After 3.7 miles of general descent, you reach Fishermans Camp, a former drive-in campground once accessible by many miles of bad road. Today the site,

distinguished by its parklike setting amid a live-oak grove, serves as a fine wilderness campsite for an overnight backpack trip (a wilderness permit is required for this). Its name hints of the fishing opportunities afforded by nearby San Mateo Creek during and after the rainy season.

At Fishermans Camp, three other trails diverge. Fishermans Camp Trail (the old road to the camp) travels east uphill to Old Tenaja Road. The San Mateo Canyon Trail, a narrow footpath, continues upstream to meet Old Tenaja Road and downstream many miles to the east boundary of Camp Pendleton.

Trip 3: Fishermans Camp Loop

Distance	5.0 miles
Total Elevation Gain/Loss	550'/550'
Hiking Time	2½ hours
Optional Maps	USGS 7.5-min *Sitton Peak*; Cleveland National Forest San Mateo Canyon Wilderness map
Best Times	November through May
Agency	CNF/TD
Difficulty	★★

After a good rain, upper San Mateo Canyon brims with cold, sparkling water. If you come on a sunny winter day, you can often enjoy a couple of hours of very comfortable, almost summer-like temperatures. By midafternoon low sunlight floods the canyon, and you may be tempted to slide into one of the shallow pools for a quick cooling-off.

A good starting point for this loop hike is a small parking area along "old" (unpaved) Tenaja Road, 3 miles north of Tenaja Station. From here an old road, reverted to a hiking trail, descends to the abandoned Fishermans Camp, a former drive-in campground, 1.5 miles away. The camp lies at the mouth of Tenaja Canyon,

whose linear alignment is associated with a rift called the Tenaja Fault.

Beautifully shaded by oaks and sycamores, Fishermans Camp is an idyllic and practical setting for a trail camp. Camp stoves can be used in one of the large bare patches amid the knee-high grass (remember—no campfires allowed). Water in Tenaja Canyon trickles by (winter and spring) on its way to the bottom of San Mateo Canyon, just 300 yards north.

A restful pause at this seductive spot is alone worth the trip, but there's more to see ahead. Find the narrow trail going north (just east of the brook in Tenaja Canyon) toward boulder-strewn, vegetation-choked San Mateo Canyon. There you will

come to a junction with the San
Mateo Canyon Trail, on the far
(west) side of the streamcourse.

Go right and follow the
trail generally northeast up San
Mateo Canyon onto a brushy
slope, around the mouth of a
prominent side canyon, and then
across a grassy bench. Ahead lie
three more creek crossings and a
couple of passages through live
oaks and chaparral. Several shallow pools, set amid colorful
metamorphic slabs, may be visited. Spring wildflowers include
bush lupine, snapdragon penstemon, monkeyflowers of various
hues, paintbrush, owl's clover,
and wild morning glory. Yuccas
send up their candle-like flower
stalks along the hillsides.

After the fourth creek
crossing, the trail sticks to the
right bank until, 1.9 miles from
Fisherman's Camp, you arrive at the Tenaja
Falls Trail, right below old Tenaja Road.

Tenaja Creek

Close the loop by walking 1.5 miles on old
Tenaja Road back to your car.

Trip 4: Upper San Mateo Canyon

Distance	7.0 miles (to Lunch Rock and back)
Total Elevation Gain/Loss	800'/800'
Hiking Time	4 hours (round trip)
Recommended Maps	USGS 7.5-min *Sitton Peak*; Cleveland National Forest San Mateo Canyon Wilderness map
Best Times	November through May
Agency	CNF/TD
Difficulty	★★★

With no roads and only the barest
hint of a trail in view, San Mateo Canyon's
inner depths are the essence of wilderness.
The sky above is bluest blue, and the air is
alive with moist, woodsy odors. The canyon walls resonate with gurgling water.
Papery sycamore leaves chafe on the wind,

and birds flit noisily about, staking out ter-
ritory in brush and tree tops. Under the
shade of live oaks, Indian *morteros* pock a
granite slab. In the stream below, pond
turtles hitching rides on the current careen
from rock to rock. A gopher snake on the
bank slithers through dry grass in search

of a small, furry meal. Only the passing of high-flying aircraft gives evidence of the outside world a few miles away.

Following the canyon may be a bit problematical. You'll be tracing the latest incarnation of the San Mateo Canyon Trail, originally constructed before the turn of the century. Trail maintenance is occasional and minimal. Floods routinely obliterate the trail where it passes close to the

Boulders at Lunch Rock area on San Mateo Creek

creekbed, and rapid regeneration of riparian vegetation and grasses tends to conceal what remains. Poison oak, nettles, and other irritating plants abound along the streambed, so wear long pants in these areas.

Begin, as in Trip 3 above, by dropping down to Fishermans Camp at the mouth of Tenaja Canyon. This is the site of one of several primitive fishing camps that lined San Mateo Canyon fifty or more years ago. During a series of wet winters in the 1930s, steelhead (sea-running rainbow trout) ran upstream to spawn in San Mateo Canyon's middle and upper reaches. Another run occurred in 1969, and more could take place during future heavy flows.

From the west edge of the grassy, oak-bowered clearing at Fishermans Camp, find the foot trail through ceanothus and scrub oak that rises onto the south wall of San Mateo Canyon. This part of the trail avoids a narrow, vegetation-choked section of the canyon about 200 feet below. After 0.4 mile you round a bend and drop quickly down 10 switchbacks to the bottom of San Mateo Canyon. Next you face a 200-yard passage through a veritable jungle of ferns, poison oak, and wild berry vines. After that you come to a creek crossing. Wade through, or skip across on the stones. From now on stay on the right (north) bank as you continue downstream.

The next ¼ mile or so of trail may be washed out. An easy scramble gets you over a low outcropping of crumbling metamorphic rock on the right. Then, as the canyon widens, the trail diverges from the stream a little and traverses an oak-dotted *potrero* ("pasture," or grassy area). About 0.5 mile past the creek crossing, the trail dips to cross two shallow stream bottoms (usually dry) just below the mouth of Bluewater Canyon. Just beyond the second wash is a signed junction with the Bluewater Trail. Stay left

and continue for another 0.7 mile down-canyon to a rough stretch where the walls pinch in and the water slides over car-sized boulders and gathers in languid pools (950 feet elevation). About 50 square miles of watershed lie upstream of this point. A large flat-topped rock, dubbed "Lunch Rock" by hikers, overlooks the stream here. You've come 3.5 miles from the trailhead at old Tenaja Road, probably the farthest you would want to venture in a single day. After sunning, swimming, eating, and a siesta, it's uphill all the way back.

For backpackers, San Mateo Canyon offers a number of pleasant campsites. Dry, sandy benches along the wider parts of the canyon abound. The following is a description of what lies beyond Lunch Rock.

Immediately down-canyon from Lunch Rock, travel is impeded by big boulders and dense growths of cattails, wild grape vines, blackberry vines, stinging nettles, mule fat, and willow saplings. Pieces of the old trail can be found away from the stream, but they often lead into impenetrable brush thickets. Wading the creek is often faster. At the 800-foot contour (4.7 miles from old Tenaja Road), there's a fine swimming hole, about 5 feet deep, set amid outcrops of dark gray metamorphic rock. Near Nickel Canyon, 5.3 miles, progress is speedier as you pick up the bed of an old mining road.

At 5.9 miles you reach a junction with the west branch of the Clark Trail. A side trip up this trail (a gain of 1300 feet in 1.3 miles) would take you to Indian Potrero, a bald area on the north ridge overlooking San Mateo Canyon. The other roads and trails to Indian Potrero come from Camp Pendleton or from private lands with no public access.

Beyond the Clark Trail junction lies an even more beautiful section of San Mateo Canyon, covered in Trip 6 below.

Trip 5: Bluewater Traverse

Distance	12.7 miles
Total Elevation Gain/Loss	2450'/2900'
Hiking Time	7 hours
Recommended Maps	USGS 7.5-min *Sitton Peak*; Cleveland National Forest San Mateo Canyon Wilderness map
Best Times	November through May
Agency	CNF/TD
Difficulty	★★★★

From Ortega Highway on the north to Tenaja Road on the south, this route traverses the heart of the San Mateo Wilderness by way of old roads and primitive trails. Carry a full backpack and plan to spend a night out in Oak Flats or San Mateo Canyon, or go light and make this simply a long day's outing. Without a doubt, March and April are the most rewarding times: knee-high grasses ripple across the potreros, chaparral blooms release their potent fragrances, and water trickles down the shady ravines.

You begin at the San Juan Loop trailhead on Ortega Highway and end at the Fishermans Camp Trailhead on "old" Tenaja Road. Transportation arrangements are a little awkward. The two trailheads are about an hour's drive apart. High-clearance 4-wheel-drive vehicles may negotiate the Killen Trail-Wildomar Road route around the east side of the wilderness. Other vehicles should stick to the longer but less bone-jarring route via Clinton Keith Road and Tenaja Road.

From the Ortega Oaks Store follow the Bear Canyon Trail (see Area M-2, Trip

San Mateo Creek near Nickel Canyon

Oak Flats

11) south to Pigeon Spring and Four Corners (3.2 miles). From Four Corners there are two routes leading into San Mateo Canyon. On the left (southeast) is the Tenaja Trail, monotonously following the spine of a treeless ridge all the way to the canyon. Our way, the Verdugo Trail straight ahead (southwest), is much more interesting.

For a mile or so the Verdugo Trail winds along steep, brushy slopes offering excellent views of the San Mateo Canyon drainage and the rounded Santa Margarita Mountains to the south. Passing over the shoulder of a ridge, the roadbed suddenly drops about 400 feet to cross an oak-shaded tributary of Bluewater Canyon (4.7 miles). Winding upward, then down again you reach, around 5.5 miles, the edge of a pleasant woodland—several hundred rolling acres shaded by live oaks and tall chaparral. At 5.8 miles, bear left and follow the Bluewater Trail east and south past Serrano Spring and Garcia Spring in the Oak Flats area.

Oak Flats is one of the nicest back corners of the Trabuco District, containing a charming mixture of oak-rimmed potreros and deeply shaded ravines. Until recently, some Scottish Highlander cattle used these meadows as grazing grounds. Meadow wildflowers include owl's clover, lupine, blue-eyed grass, and some non-natives typically found in formerly grazed areas: filaree and scarlet pimpernel.

A fairly complete reconnaissance of the Oak Flats area might include a visit to nearby peak 2616, overlooking the private Rancho Carrillo development in Verdugo Potrero (an area well within the overall outlines of, but excluded from San Mateo Canyon Wilderness by a "cherry-stem" boundary). The coastline is only 13 air-miles away from here, and the wide, blue arc of the Pacific Ocean can be seen on most days.

During winter and spring, water trickles down the ravine containing Serrano and Garcia springs, and flows onward toward Nickel Canyon. With purification, it can be used by backpackers camping overnight in the area.

Beyond Oak Flats, the poor roadbed that has so far served as the Bluewater Trail veers left (southeast) and attains a nearly barren summit (7.5 miles). After about 250 yards, the roadbed turns southwest, while the Bluewater Trail (a footpath) continues southeast, descending gradually toward Bluewater Canyon, 1500 feet below. After a short, confusing stretch through a grassy area, the route pitches very sharply downward down a brushy ridgeline. Newer switchbacks do little to keep the feet from sliding; backpackers may at times feel safer sliding down on the seat of the pants! There's a short respite about halfway down, followed by gentler switchbacks down to the bottom of the canyon (9.0 miles).

After the effort of descent, the cold, bubbling stream in Bluewater Canyon is the hiker's equivalent of paradise. Small oaks and sycamores provide semi-shade. The Bluewater Trail, overgrown by small shrubs and grasses, continues downstream on the banks for 0.8 mile, crossing the creek several times.

Don't miss the obscure junction with the San Mateo Canyon Trail on a bench at Bluewater Canyon's mouth (9.8 miles). Turn left here and work your way east along the left side of San Mateo Canyon. Just beyond the creek crossing (10.5 miles) pick up the series of switchbacks leading toward Fishermans Camp and "old" Tenaja Road 1.5 miles beyond it (see Trips 3 and 4).

Opposite the creek crossing, on the nose of a long ridge leading north, you'll spot the switchbacks of the Tenaja Trail, which leads back to Four Corners. If you want to loop back to Ortega Highway, this is the expedient way to go.

Trip 6: Clark Trail to Lower San Mateo Canyon

Distance	6.0 miles
Total Elevation Gain/Loss	1700'/1700'
Hiking Time	4 hours (round trip)
Recommended Maps	USGS 7.5-min *Margarita Peak*; Cleveland National Forest San Mateo Canyon Wilderness map
Best Times	November through May
Agency	CNF/TD
Difficulty	★★★

The east branch of the Clark Trail visits two canyons, as different in character as night and day. The first, Cold Spring Canyon (not to be confused with the canyon of the same name in Caspers Park), is cool, dark, and somber; only a few sunbeams are admitted through the oaks and sycamores clustered along the tiny stream. The second, the lower part of San Mateo Canyon, is warm, bright, and cheery. Here, the creek dances over sun-warmed granite and swirls through shallow pools.

The trek down the Clark Trail requires long pants to fend off encroaching poison oak and chaparral, and sturdy shoes for stability on the steep grades. Reaching the trailhead may prove to be challenging, too. The access road passes through two inholdings bordering San Mateo Canyon Wilderness. The owners of these properties have intermittently permitted passage for hikers and vehicles across their land in the past. Check with the Trabuco District office (see Appendix 5) to see if access is possible and to get an update on the condition of the trail.

From the end of the paved Tenaja Road continue a short way on dirt to a 4-

way intersection of dirt roads. Continue straight. After 0.6 mile, make a sharp right, turning away from the locked ranch gate straight ahead. Continue 3.2 miles on a poor road (high clearance recommended; may be impassable in wet weather) to a gate at Cold Spring Ranch. Continue for another 0.7 mile to a clearing at the road's end, where the Clark Trail begins.

The trail, actually the eroded bed of an old mining road, drops steadily along a north-facing slope thickly covered with mature (probably 60 years old) mixed chaparral: toyon, scrub oak, sugar bush, and various ceanothus shrubs grown to heights of 15 feet. After the winter rains, tendrils of wild cucumber and clematis vines probe the dense canopy; while wood fern, squaw bush, poison oak, gooseberry, currant, and a dozen varieties of colorful wildflowers form a dense understory.

After 0.5 mile, you arrive at the bottom of Cold Spring Canyon, pleasantly resounding with the murmur of a trickling stream. As you continue down-canyon on the trail, you pass under a lacy net of oak and sycamore limbs. Clusters of giant chain fern, rampant growths of poison oak, and thickets of bracken fern conceal all but the narrow tread of the trail. The rusted hulk of a circa-1950 automobile lies in the streambed at one of the trail crossings, half-buried in silt. Two more old autos lie concealed nearby, marooned on a road that no longer exists.

During a trip through the gloomiest part of this canyon, my attention was caught by a soft, rustling noise emanating from the ground all around me. It was literally hundreds of Coast Range newts groping through the leaf litter beside the stream.

At 1.2 miles (from the parking area), the trail crosses the stream for the last time and starts to climb the north wall of the canyon. Here the sunstruck slopes are clothed in a somewhat sparse cover of mostly sage-scrub vegetation: black sage, white sage, California sagebrush, buckwheat, laurel sumac, chamise, deerweed, and yucca.

Well-crafted, mortarless stonework has kept the trail from slipping away

San Mateo Creek

downslope, even though the bed is littered with jagged shards of metamorphic rock fallen from the old roadcuts. At 1.8 miles the trail tops out and then contours across a rocky knob on the ridge dividing Cold Spring and San Mateo canyons. The northern San Diego County coastline may be seen, as well as parts of Camp Pendleton.

Immediately below you is the confluence of Devil and Cold Spring canyons, both seemingly impenetrable from this vantage point. These canyons were the scene of a celebrated bear chase back in 1899. In that year two hunters from San Juan Capistrano, accompanied by a trained greyhound, set off to destroy a rogue grizzly known locally as "the big bear." Like most of the few remaining California grizzlies, this one had a habit of drifting out of the mountains occasionally and raiding the local ranches and apiaries. The chase continued east up lower San Mateo Canyon, Devil Canyon, and Cold Spring Canyon, then south and west past Margarita Peak to the headwaters of San Onofre Creek in today's Camp Pendleton. There, after 36 hours of hot pursuit, the bear succumbed to a hail of bullets. (After receiving the skull and the field measurements, scientists at the Smithsonian Institution estimated the bear's standing height at over 9 feet, and its weight at over 1400 pounds. The skull, on deposit in the Smithsonian today, is the largest of any California grizzly on record.)

Beyond the rocky knob, the trail pitches downward, first gently and then very sharply, into San Mateo Canyon. The chaparral vegetation is again taller and denser, providing intermittent shade on the way down. At the bottom (3.0 miles), a pleasant, oak-dotted glade next to the streamside—the first reasonably large place to set up an overnight camp—awaits you. From this point, you can explore either upstream or downstream.

Downstream 0.4 mile is a narrow section of canyon lined with sycamores and alders, and containing some fine pools. Sunbathing on the smooth rocks is great anytime, but the water becomes quite stagnant by midsummer. Sound effects come from the rock-ribbed cliff nearby: the hootings of owls and the trills of canyon wrens. Small fish, frogs, and newts are seen in and around the water. The bears are gone, but quite frequently mountain lions pass this way. Below the pools, you may continue down the meandering course of the creek, but not beyond the gauging station (2 miles below the pools) that marks Camp Pendleton's boundary.

In the upstream direction you can ramble an easy mile along the bed of an old mining road, spotting evidence of the mining days—old rusted equipment and a tumbledown hut—in the shade of the oaks. See Trip 4 for a description of San Mateo Canyon above this point. With a car shuttle, you could loop back through San Mateo Canyon all the way to old Tenaja Road, a long and difficult trek easily beyond the scope of a single day's hike.

Appendix 1: Best Hikes

Best Beach Hike
- **San Onofre State Beach** (Area B-5, Trip 2). Here the primeval Southern California coastline survives more or less intact.

Best Suburban Hikes
- **El Moro Canyon Loop** (Area B-3, Trip 4). Ocean views and passages through dark, spooky oak groves.
- **Telegraph Canyon Traverse** (Area F-l, Trip 8). Miles of oak-dotted hills and gentle canyons.
- **Oak Canyon Nature Center** (Area F-2, Trip 1). An agreeable patch of wilderness amidst the wilds of suburban Anaheim.
- **Borrego Canyon to Red Rock** (Area F-3, Trip 1). Shady canyon and eroded sandstone cliffs.
- **Arroyo Trabuco** (Area F-4, Trip 3). A still-wild coastal canyon filled with sycamores and oaks.

Best Mountain Hikes
- **Holy Jim Falls** (Area M-1, Trip 11). An intimate canyon setting highlighted by a picturesque little waterfall.
- **Fishermans Camp Loop** (Area M-3, Trip 3). A pleasant ramble among oaks and wildflowers along San Mateo Creek.

Best Canyon Hikes
- **Lower Hot Spring Canyon** (Area M-2, Trip 9). Narrow, rugged, and sublime. Difficulties and hazards discourage most hikers from penetrating very far.
- **Upper San Mateo Canyon** (Area M-3, Trip 4). The best-preserved major watercourse in the Santa Ana Mountains.

Best Waterfalls
- **Lower Hot Spring Canyon** (Area M-2, Trip 9). Water falls 140 feet—Orange County's tallest. Remote, and inaccessible to the average hiker.

- **Tenaja Falls** (Area M-3, Trip 1). A multitiered cascade hewn in polished granite. Easy to reach.

Best View Hikes
- **Emerald Vista Point** (Area B-3, Trip 3). Bird's-eye view of Orange County's coast and the offshore islands.
- **Santiago Peak** (Area M-1, Trip 12). 100-mile views encompassing most of coastal southern California.

Best Wildflowers
- **Mesa Loop** (Area F-5, Trip 6). Spring flowers of the sage-scrub, chaparral and oak-woodland plant communities.
- **Santa Rosa Plateau Loop** (Area F-6, Trip 2). Catch some of California's finest springtime displays of greenery and wildflowers in March or April.
- **San Juan Loop Trail** (Area M-2, Trip 2). Wildflowers of the mountain meadows and chaparral.
- **Bluewater Traverse** (Area M-3, Trip 5). Wildflowers of the chaparral and potrero country.

Best Autumn Colors
- **Trabuco Canyon** (Area M-1, Trip 14). Tawny colors of willow, sycamore, and maple. Best in December.

Best Bird and Wildlife Watching
- **San Joaquin Freshwater Marsh Reserve** (Area B-2, Trip 2). Local as well as migrant bird life. Tour or special permit required for entry.
- **Bell Canyon** (Area F-5, Trips 2, 3, 4, & 5). Deer, bobcats, and mountain lions frequent this area.
- **Chiquito Basin** (Area M-2, Trip 4). A sunny, oak-rimmed valley; a natural pasture.
- **San Mateo Canyon** (Area M-3, all trips). Aquatic, oak woodland, and chaparral habitats attract a wide variety of reptiles, amphibians, birds and mammals.

Best Mountain Biking and Running Trails

- **El Moro Canyon** (Area B-3, Trip 4). Up El Moro Canyon and back is easy and delightful. A loop via Red Tail Ridge is much more difficult.
- **Gilman Peak** (Area F-1, Trip 2). A short but challenging ascent on a graded roadway. Excellent views at the top.
- **Telegraph Canyon Traverse** (Area F-1, Trip 8). Moderate grades. Remarkably unspoiled, yet close to the city's edge.
- **Whiting Ranch Loop** (Area F-3, Trip 2). Moderate grades on mostly wide trails. Fast becoming a classic among mountain bikers.
- **Aliso/Wood Canyons** (Area B-4, Trip 2). Probably the most popular spot for mountain biking in Orange County. Mountain bikers must stay on designated routes.
- **North Main Divide Traverse** (Area M-1, Trip 3). Challenging trip up and over the northern crest of the Main Divide. Delightful views.
- **Harding Road** (Area M-1, Trips 8 & 9). Long climb to the Main Divide just north of Old Saddleback. Return the same way or continue along the Main Divide.
- **Indian Truck Trail** (Area M-1, Trip 13). The most scenic ascent by road to the Main Divide from the east.

Appendix 2: Urban and Regional Trails

Despite its automobile-dominated milieu, Orange County has made significant strides in the development of alternative transportation systems. Already in place are the rudiments of what promises to be one of the finest regional trail systems in the United States for cyclists, walkers, and equestrians.

Cyclists and walkers, for example, can explore many miles of paved pathways along Orange County's beachfront and several of its watercourses: the Santa Ana River, San Diego Creek (north from Upper Newport Bay), San Juan Creek (through San Juan Capistrano), and the former Anaheim Union Canal (the El Cajon Trail in Yorba Linda). These "river" trails, typically following nearly flat levees, allow fairly pleasant travel through some of the county's most densely populated areas.

Orange County's general plan recognizes the importance of setting aside parcels of land for future parks, open space, and trail corridors along its rapidly urbanizing south and east fringes. County policy, in fact, specifically requires that developers of large-scale projects dedicate substantial parcels of land for recreational purposes in exchange for the right to build. The riding-and-hiking-trail element of the general plan has identified 45 regional trails (more than 300 miles), targeted for completion by the early years of the next century.

In the next decade, efforts will be devoted to linking the newer county trails with existing truck roads and trails in the Santa Ana Mountains part of Cleveland National Forest. When completed as envisioned, the regional trail network will feature at least five distinct routes spanning the county from the coast to the mountains.

Riverside County, too, is acquiring open space and has defined a regional trail system. Orange County's Santa Ana River Trail now extends east into Riverside's Santa Ana River Regional Park. Another trail, to be constructed atop an abandoned railroad bed parallel to Interstate 15, will link Corona and Lake Elsinore. As suburban development proceeds along that corridor, easements will be set aside for trails leading west into Cleveland National Forest.

Since the trips in this book were selected on the basis of being "afield," i.e., away from populated areas, as well as being suitable for travel "afoot," I did not highlight many worthy urban and semi-urban trails in Orange County. More information about Orange County's regional trail system may be obtained by contacting the Harbors, Beaches, and Parks division of Orange County's Environmental Management Agency: 1 Irvine Park Road, Orange, CA 92669; (714) 771-6731 or (714) 834-2400.

Appendix 3: Recommended Reading

Bailey, H.P., *The Climate of Southern California*, University of California Press, 1966.

Bakker, Elna, *An Island Called California*, 2nd edition, University of California Press, 1984.

Belzer, Thomas J., *Roadside Plants of Southern California*, Mountain Press Publishing Co., 1984.

California Coastal Commission, *California Coastal Access Guide*, 3rd edition, University of California Press, 1983.

California Division of Mines and Geology, Geologic Map of California—Santa Ana Sheet, 1965.

Cleveland National Forest (recreation map), 1994.

Croker, Ken, *Santa Ana Mountains Trail Guide*, 4th edition, Whale and Eagle Publishing Co., 1991.

Friis, Leo J., *Orange County through Four Centuries*, Pioneer Press. 1965. (Out of print)

Hallan-Gibson, Pamela, *The Golden Promise: An Illustrated History of Orange County*, Windsor Publications, 1986.

Jaeger, Edmond C. and Smith, Arthur C., *Introduction to the Natural History of Southern California*, University of California Press, 1971.

Leadabrand, Russ, *Guidebook to the Mountains of San Diego and Orange Counties*, Ward Ritchie Press, 1971. (Out of print)

McPherson, Alan, *Nature Walks in Orange County*, Bear Flag Books, 1990.

Meadows, Don, *Historic Place Names in Orange County*, Paisano Press, 1966. (Out of print)

Munz, Philip A., *California Spring Wildflowers*, University of California Press, 1961.

Munz, Philip A., *Shore Wildflowers of California, Oregon and Washington*, University of California Press, 1964.

National Geographic Society, *Field Guide to the Birds of North America*, 2nd edition, 1987.

Peterson, P. Victor, *Native Trees of Southern California*, University of California Press, 1966.

Rasmussen, Robert, *Mountain Biking the Coast Range: Orange County and Cleveland National Forest*, 2nd edition, Fine Edge Productions, 1995.

Raven, Peter H., *Native Shrubs of Southern California*, University of California Press, 1966.

Russo, Ron and Olhausen, Pam, *Pacific Intertidal Life*, Nature Study Guild, 1981.

Schad, Jerry, *Afoot and Afield in Los Angeles County*, Wilderness Press, 1991.

——, *Afoot and Afield in San Diego County*, 2nd edition, Wilderness Press, 1992.

——, *Cycling Orange County*, Centra Publications, 1989.

Schultz, Elizabeth, (ed.), *Visiting Orange County's Past*, Orange County Historical Commission, 1984.

Sharp, Robert P., *Coastal Southern California* (geology guide), Kendall/Hunt Publishing Company, 1978.

Sharp, Robert P., *Geology Field Guide to Southern California*, William C. Brown Co., 1972.

Jim Sleeper, *2nd Orange County Almanac of Historical Oddities*, Ocusa Press, 1974. (Out of print)

Jim Sleeper, *A Grizzly Introduction to the Santa Ana Mountains*, California Classics, 1976. (Out of print)

Stephenson, Terry E., *Shadows of Old Saddleback*, (reprint of 1931 edition), Rasmussen Press, 1974. (Out of print)

Appendix 4: Local Organizations

Audubon Society, Sea and Sage Chapter
P.O. Box 5447
Irvine, CA 92616
(949) 261-7963
(Sponsors field trips and bird walks in Orange County's coastal wetlands and foothill canyons)

Sierra Club, Orange County Group
230 E. 17th St., Suite 206
Costa Mesa, CA 92627
(949) 631-3140
(Sponsors day hikes and backpacks throughout Orange County; plans and maintains trails in the Trabuco District of Cleveland National Forest)

Amigos de Bolsa Chica
16531 Bolsa Chica St., Suite 312
Huntington Beach, CA 92649
(714) 840-1575
(Activities associated with Bolsa Chica Ecological Reserve)

Crystal Cove Interpretive Association
P.O. Box 4352
Laguna Beach, CA 92652
(949) 494-3539
(Activities associated with Crystal Cove State Park)

Chino Hills State Park Interpretive Association
4195 Chino Hills Parkway, Suite E-454
Chino Hills, CA 91709
(Activities associated with Chino Hills State Park)

The Nature Conservancy of California
1400 Quail St., Suite 130
Newport Beach, CA 92660
(949) 263-0933
(Manages and sponsors guided hikes on Nature Conservancy and Irvine Company open-space reserves in and near Orange County)

Appendix 5: Information Sources

Parks, Preserves, and Agencies

Aliso/Wood Canyons Regional Park (AWCRP)
(949) 831-2791

Bolsa Chica Ecological Reserve (BCER)
(714) 846-1114

Carbon Canyon Regional Park (CCRP)
4442 Carbon Canyon Road
Brea, CA 92621
(949) 996-5252

Crystal Cove State Park (CCSP)
c/o Orange Coast District
18331 Enterprise Lane
Huntington Beach, CA 92648
(949) 494-3539 or (949) 492-0802

Chino Hills State Park (CHSP)
15838 Pomona-Rincon Road
P.O. Box 2163
Chino, CA 91708
(909) 780-6222

Cleveland National Forest
Trabuco Ranger District (CNF/TD)
1147 E. Sixth Street
Corona, CA 91719
(909) 736-1811

Cleveland National Forest
El Cariso Visitor Information Office
32353 Ortega Highway
Lake Elsinore, CA 92330
(909) 678-3700

Caspers Wilderness Park (CWP)
33401 Ortega Highway
San Juan Capistrano, CA 92675
(949) 728-0235

Irvine Regional Park (IRP)
1 Irvine Park Road
Orange, CA 92669
(714) 633-8074

Orange County Environmental Management Agency (OCEMA)
Harbors, Beaches and Parks
(714) 771-6731 or (714) 834-2400

Oak Canyon Nature Center (OCNC)
6700 Walnut Canyon Road
Anaheim, CA
(714) 998-8380

O'Neill Regional Park (ONRP)
30892 Trabuco Canyon Road
Trabuco Canyon, CA 92678
(949) 858-9365

San Clemente State Beach (SCSB)
225 Avenida Calafia
San Clemente, CA 92672
(949) 492-3156 or (949) 492-0802

San Joaquin Freshwater Marsh Reserve (SJFMR)
Department of Ecology and Evolutionary Biology
University of California
Irvine, CA 92717
(949) 824-6031 or (949) 824-6006

Santiago Oaks Regional Park (SORP)
2145 N. Windes Drive
Orange, CA 92669
(714) 538-4400

San Onofre State Beach (SOSB)
c/o Pendleton Coast Area
3030 Avenida del Presidente
San Clemente, CA 92672
(949) 492-4872 or (949) 492-0802

Santa Rosa Plateau Ecological Reserve (SRPER)
22115 Tenaja Road
Murrieta, CA 92362
(909) 677-6951

Tucker Wildlife Sanctuary
29322 Modjeska Canyon Road
Orange, CA 92667
(714) 649-2760

Upper Newport Bay Ecological Reserve (UNBER)
(949) 640-1751

Whiting Ranch Wilderness Park (WRWP)
(949) 589-4729

Map Sources

Adventure 16
1959 Harbor Blvd.
Costa Mesa, CA 92627
(949) 650-3301

Allied Map Services
966 North Main
Orange, CA 92667
(714) 532-4300

Recreational Equipment, Inc.
1411 S. Village Way
Santa Ana, CA 92705
(714) 543-4142

Western Map Company
1370 Brea Blvd.
Fullerton, CA 92835
(714) 525-2315

Cleveland National Forest
—see previous section

Index